Majid Naeemi Nabatian

Savalan

Majid Naeemi Nabatian

Savalan

JustFiction Edition

Imprint
Any brand names and product names mentioned in this book are subject to trademark, brand or patent protection and are trademarks or registered trademarks of their respective holders. The use of brand names, product names, common names, trade names, product descriptions etc. even without a particular marking in this work is in no way to be construed to mean that such names may be regarded as unrestricted in respect of trademark and brand protection legislation and could thus be used by anyone.

Cover image: www.ingimage.com

Publisher:
JustFiction! Edition
is a trademark of
Dodo Books Indian Ocean Ltd., member of the OmniScriptum S.R.L Publishing group
str. A.Russo 15, of. 61, Chisinau-2068, Republic of Moldova Europe
Printed at: see last page
ISBN: 978-620-3-57838-6

In the Name of God

***Book name**: Savalan*

***Genre**: Tragedy- Romance*

***Author**: Majid NaeemiNabatian*

Summary: Sam, the main character of this story, meets Helena accidentally. After lots of challenges they face, finally Helena has to leave the country and Sam's painful destiny makes the readers of this story think. Social conflicts and romantic challenges for the characters occur based on what happens to the characters!!

Sam saves the life of a street cat and takes care of it. The cat is named Sami and dies before the bitter destiny of Sam. After that, Sam dies at a young age because of an adverse accident and the other character of the story, Helena, who saw Sam as a savior feels very lonely!!!! Farhad, the other character of the story, who is one of the very close friends of Sam proposes to Helena. So, Helena trusts him and accepts the proposal but!!! Farhad's father disagrees strictly. Helena travels to the US and stays there for a long time. During these years, Helena is unaware of Farhad. She marries in the US and gives birth to a baby. After 30 years, Helena's husband dies and she decides to return to her homeland with her son who is now a well-educated young guy. When Helena returns to her homeland, she goes to Sam's tomb to meet him again! This was the summary of this story and you are invited to read the novel thoroughly.

Sincerely,

Majid Naeemi Nabatian

Introduction

Since the heroes of our lives have always had constructive signs in the imaginary or real worlds, thus a positive trait can be found in every hero.

I have to say that I decided to write and use the greatness of these Aryan people and these heroes. I decided to imagine an example of the sweetness and bitterness of the real or even unreal world of such heroes. Whether in my own mind and their minds, writing a long novel takes a lot of time and it is as if the writer searches his life in the imaginations of himself and others. He considers the intellectual imaginations of all classes through the standpoint of the people who are drowned in social life and also through the movies he watches or the stories he reads. However, he is unaware of the mind of those living in far lands and it needs travelling. I have travelled to the countries near Iran as much as I could and I am somehow familiar with their culture. To me, the most interesting point was the cultural distance between Iran and these countries around us. It was manifested in civilization, language, science, philosophy, etc.

In fact, my homeland, Iran, has a vast degree of civilization, culture, and complete beauty from the south to the north. I think life is like a novel, both real and unreal, and human realizes that he has had a sweet dream and now he just woke up to step into a real world when he says goodbye to his dependent world. Here sleep means a deep understanding on the path of reading a novel.

At the end of winter

I look outside at the yard

At the cherry tree that

Has lost its leaves sooner than expected!

But it is the season of life, here…

The sweet light of love is shining instead of snow and blizzard

Life finds its own beauty

Even for me when I am sitting alone in my room

This is life, just like the cherry tree in the yard

That spreads its roots first and then grows

And has fruits in maturity

And loses its leaves in fall

It is bent down in winter…

I wish it was spring all the time

My share from this short life

Was love and staying in love

3

Winter is beautiful but when it goes
Its cold sorrow stays with me
My pen cannot write the moments of winter
My departure does not respond to my sorrow
I have come to you again and am looking at you
Oh spring! I am tired of the early fall leaves
Of stress, of distress, of these hundredths of a second
Which pass cold like winter…
You look is my matter of delight, I am completely happy with the sky
Which is the most beautiful roof I have!
The velvet look of green trees reminds the old man of
The adolescence and life
Perhaps there is a city behind the sky, our city is there
I leave to say the unsaid things to you
You are naïve and I am honest, I am a simple passerby
Who looks at you…
The color of my face has lots of words with you
Your silence is wavy
I cannot stop thinking about it
Maybe everyone is alone
They look at you with eyes full of words
I say my words to you with the ink of my pen
I am like you
I have built a house behind my texts
I know this privacy and this life
What a winter and what a spring are always flowing
And time is passing…

When they talked about humanity and love, everyone laughed and when I talked about humanity and love, this time everyone laughed at me too! The natural life of human is now a mechanical life. We have to become iron based on this mechanical life! What a pity that this world has tuned me…

Chapter One

Life is a work in our minds and hearts just like a portrait which is full of joy but a bit pain and wound has surrounded it. Its concept is just in the mind of the creator of this work.

And sometimes in the mind of its audience…

It was 12:00 p.m. of a semi-hot day in fall. Sam was finishing his first grade in elementary school. Those were good days for Sam. The class was over and he said goodbye to his teacher like his other classmates and then he left the classroom and then left the school. The school was closed. On the way home, he thought about going to his father's supermarket which was a few steps farther than the school to drink a cold cola and then go home. Sam's father was sorting out the stuff in the supermarket. As he saw his son, he stopped working. Father: hi my son, are you ok? How was the school? Sam: hi, I missed you actually, so I decided to come see you and take a cold cola out of the refrigerator and then go home. It can be said that Sam had strange thoughts in his mind since the childhood! Perhaps nobody could be aware of such thoughts but according to his family, he was a stupid and bad-tempered boy! Days and years were passing. Sam was growing with the same introversion. Their house was at the same school where Sam was studying. His father was a janitor at that school and could open a supermarket outside of the school by saving the money he had earned at the coffee shop inside the school. However, he could not earn enough money for his seven-member family. Sam had two other brothers and two sisters. His parents were totally kind and hard-working. Because of the job of Sam's father, their living place was changed once every two years and Sam and his family entered a new environment for living… for this reason, it can be said that Sam grew in completely different conditions compared to his friends. He passed his elementary school under difficult conditions and entered a secondary school at the best neighborhood of their city. The principals of that school had provided the best educational conditions for the students of that school and it had happened because Sam's father was the janitor of that school! His workplace had been transferred to the new school with good conditions!! At that time, Sam's father got completely broke at the supermarket and had nothing… due to his debt, he had turned into a fugitive and these problems had left negative and adverse effects on the family, especially Sam.

It was the end of winter and the weather was extremely cold.

Sam was studying at the last grade of secondary school. He was sitting in the class and staring at his teacher. He was concentrating on the lesson to learn it perfectly but his innocent look showed that he was thinking about the house and did not want to go back to the house where his father was hiding by force! And his mother who was worried about the future… His siblings had a weird fear of life on their faces.

Their father's debts had become a big problem to them, so that the life had become bitter than ever to this simple family. Since they were the janitor of a governmental school, the police were not allowed to enter the school and their house and Sam's father could stay at home freely!! And suffer from watching his poor family. He could not even afford buying some bread.

The school principal felt pity for this family and helped them with a little money, but the creditors came to the school with the police every day. Perhaps it was like a nightmare for Sam and his family, who had lived with good reputation, to see what was happening.Everyone at the school like teachers, assistant principal, and principal went to the creditors to talk and ask for a chance for Sam's father every time they came to the school accompanied by the police. But all of the creditors asked for their money and there was no chance for this family! Sam's mother became weaker and her face got more pale every day. Sam's father was the same too and they were experiencing failure every day!! The children in this family were weaker than ever with a broken heart. They were sad for their parents. The sky at night brought too much sadness for them and the sky of the day was the time for dealing with the strange problems. Sam's only friend was his tears on his cheeks and he could communicate with the drops of tears and talk about his painful unsaid words. He was at the second grade of secondary school and had a weak spirit which was broken into pieces but he decided to drop out of school. As his closest friend suggested, he went to the turning workshop of his friend's father to work. He worked there for one year as a footboy; a very difficult job that after a while, all of the boys at the neighborhood called Sam as "Asghar the oily" because of his oily and black hands. Sam was not a 17-year-old teenager with a thin body but not too very tall. It was 8:00 p.m.... and Sam was looking outside through the window. It was snowing and the beautiful night could be seen in the light of the sidewalk and street. He could enjoy watching the scene but only watching it looked beautiful because the weather was freezing outside. Suddenly, his friend's brother who was his employer there shouted: Sam come on, close all of the shutters and go home. By the way, there is nobody here tonight to help you. You must do it by yourself. 18 big shutters of 2 meters wanted to communicate deeply with Sam's frozen hands but he could not do that. However, he had to do that because of fear from a fine by his employer and then he had to go home on foot in that freezing night as soon as possible. It was the beginning of the difficulties of Sam's life. He had to accept that he was in a world where nobody was satisfied. He closed all of the shutters and then headed home. He remembered his childhood while walking in the snow and his shoulders were shivering of cold weather. He remembered the time when his father had not gotten broke yet. They had a good life and Sam had tasted the sweet taste of life next to his parents although he was a little child. The intense falling of snowflakes had hidden the tears in Sam's eyes. The pedestrians who were running home because of cold weather and snow. Sam was still walking and talking to himself and the sky. It was 7:00 a.m. when his mother with a tired and sad face comes to her son and wakes him up. She prepares him breakfast as every day so that her son, Sam, goes to work after having breakfast. The tiredness of working too much yesterday was still seen in his face but he hit his body with his fists to relax his body. A new day had begun for him. Having life is scarier and easier than staying with it or leaving it. life is the same soul... Sam had worked in several places during the last 2-3 years until he became tired of being pointless. He decided to join the military service, so he was sent to a military garrison. After finishing the military service, he began looking for a new job without having any important job background. The day he received his military service completion certificate, his look was weirdly worried about the future. He was still hopeful to make a clear future for himself. Summer days come and pass and again the cold winter approaches. Sam was depressed and sad of the tiring game of life. He spent his days and nights, looked at the clock, it was 7:00 p.m. and his only friend on those days of loneliness was a bench in the park where he went a few days every week. The cold weather of winter was the reason of empty park where there was not even a passer-by. In front of his bench outside of the park, there was a girls' school that the students got out of the school at a specific hour every day and then went home on the same sidewalk. The park, cold weather, and Sam's loneliness were his friends. He did not like to miss this peace and silence… it was 5:00 p.m. and the same students had left the school and were walking on the same sidewalk near the park, heading home. At the meantime, two of those girls entered the park in that freezing weather. The cold eyes of one of them with a strange sparkle were looking at Sam. She was amazed what he was doing there alone in that freezing weather. This also looked weird for Sam because he had never received such an attention by anyone! But as Sam raised his head, he saw that the girls looked as small as a doll along the long path in the park. After a few seconds, snowing decreased his vision and then after a few minutes, Sam felt cold. He decided to go home but on the way his mind was busy with other problems and got captivated in the thoughts of loneliness! He was looking for a window to open to the future and be hopeful for better coming days… from the next day, he decided to go to the park exactly at the hour when the school was closed and sit on the same bench to see the angel of his dreams. It was 5:10 p.m. and the school was closed but he did not see the same girl. Sam put his forehead on his both hands out of sadness. His only friend was the same cold bench of his loneliness. He welcomed the winter night with pale face and then headed home. Sam put his hand on the bench and said goodbye to the empty bench full of loneliness until they meet each other again some other time and begin the moments of loneliness by being together! On the way home, Sam saw a guy who was smoking cigarette. He was tempted to buy a cigarette but he thought: what a pity that cigarette has a short life and average height like me! And he passed that guy and walked home. He opened the house door and went straight to his room. he closed the door, lied on his bed, stared at the ceiling, and began talking to himself: dear friend who blow into my room! is this coldness of life which feels empathy with me?! Is the bench of my wishes broken by you? Or does it stand in front of you and says nothing?! My body has got used to you! And I become warm with your coldness… These were the sentences and words Sam said to the cold wind of winter!

But he received no answer. Suddenly, a cold wind blew the window firmly and opened the window. Sam realized that the wind is not a bad friend to him and his bench. Sam smiled sadly. He looked outside the window and thanked God.

He was interested in white color for no reason.

His white clothes were a sign of this interest. Perhaps he thought that white was the only color which brought him peace. He did not pay attention to other colors because he saw the world around him in different colors and considered so many colors as the reason of his problems. But he considered white color specific to some special people who lived like himself and preferred the black and white life to colorful life. He had written on the wall of his room with black pencil: I am restless and full of distress... but still think about you. His love was imaginary, as if he loved living in dreams! He was so dependent on it so that he had put a photo of himself on the wall just in case, because he had no mirror in his room to look at himself every day!

By doing so, he wanted to stop the movement of the clock hands by putting his photo on the wall!! He wanted to stop the flying of time just in his favor...! Sam was standing by the window and looking outside. He looked at a corner on the street and saw a cat which was stuck in snow under the light and was looking around. As Sam walked a few steps towards it, he realized that the left leg of the cat was hurt! He began running out of the room and the house. As he arrived at the house door, he began running towards the other side of the street. As he saw the white fluffy cat, he realized that it was limping and could not put up with the cold weather and pain. Sam tried to draw the attention of the cat to himself, so he went towards the house door and the fluffy cat also walked behind him. When the cat reached the step in front of the door, it jumped on the step with its hurt leg and went inside the house. It needed warmth and food. It was just like Sam! Lonely... Sam talked to the lonely cat and it was as if the cat understood him. Sam gave it food and washed it with warm water and his own shampoo. At the end, he dried the cat with a small clean towel. He also used the spray which he used for his leg and sprayed it on the cat. Then, he looked at the clean white fluffy cat and thought about the name he wanted to give it. he decided to choose a name like his own name and called the cat: Sami. He thought about building a small house for the cat and asked help from his older brother whose room was next to his room in order to build a wooden house for Sami.

Sam had not laughed wholeheartedly for many years and he had gotten used to short smiles. But when he saw that Sami was staring at him, he became so happy for a few minutes. Now, he had a new friend! Sam spent that night in a lovely relaxation for himself. It was morning. When he woke up, he saw his mother next to him. Her face was sad and it was not obvious if she was happy a lot or a new problem had just happened!! Sam: Hi!

Mother: Hi my son, Sam? I've got wonderful news for you.

Sam: what?!

Mother: a rich man who is one of the old friends of your father has met him somewhere and he has decided to help you with our debt! He wants to pay for all our debt!!

Sam was extremely happy. It was the best day of his life that was just like a dream. His eyes were tearful out of joy. Suddenly, a sound was heard from his room which was mewing. It was Sami which was sympathizing with Sam and his mother! Sam's father could pay for all of his debt with the help of his old friend. He even rented a house near the same school once they were living and Sam's family said goodbye to the life at school forever. The life of Sam and his family had transformed greatly. They could move towards happiness and peace with this change. After all of the good things which happened to Sam and his family, Sam had to do something to have a good future like other young men. He asked his father to talk to his friend and find a good job for him!! But his father gave Sam an ambiguous answer!

It had been a few days that Sam's father was quiet and depressed instead of being happy. Nobody, except Sam's mother, was aware of the reason for this sadness. Sam had noticed this story! he asked his mother to tell him the reason for his father's depression. When Sam was informed of the whole story, he stared at an unknown point and felt that it would be possible to return to their former lives or even more painful. A strange sorrow was felt in his heart. He sat sadly in front of his mother for a few minutes, put his right fingers on his forehead and closed his eyes for a second…

His father who had helped them a lot was a drug smuggler!! And worked illegally in the field of drug. For giving them money for their debt, he had received some letter of credits from Sam's father!! And he had asked his father to engage in their illegal activities in return. The only thing Sam was thinking was his father and family! He knew that it would be difficult for his father to do such a thing after living with honor for many years to destroy the future of the family. Sam's father had no choice. He would be thrown in jail if he did not accept and his family would be in danger if he told the police. That night was the most difficult night for Sam's father. His heart was beating fast. When he looked at Sam and his family, his eyes became red and tearful… life can be like a song without any sound, but whether it is short, lovely, or sad like a very long movie, we are living in one of these states and life is going on, take it or leave it…. a destructive silence had filled the house and the brothers were looking at each other. They were sad and the terror of living another horrible life was felt in their hearts. Their mother was melting like a candle, as if the whole sorrow in the world was in her heart and eyes. But the father was trying to show everything normal. Nobody was aware of his heart! He was remembering the happy days of his life when he was young… the day he fell in love and the day he married. He was young when his first child was born. He had strange thoughts for making his children happy! But now his hair was white and he had spent a bad life, he was thinking to whom he had oppressed in the past?! why would he do such an illegal thing? Why… ? At the end, he felt proud of the only thing he had in his life which was his family. His name was Iraj and no freshness and youthfulness was seen in his face anymore.

He was 64 years old but looked very old, even older than those at his age!! However, a strange masculinity was shining in his look and words could be read from his look which reflected his words in his heart, showing honesty in his behavior… He had full faith in God and his religion and it was very important for him to give halal food to his family. Nobody had ever seen his tears even in the most difficult moments of life! His eyes were red, showing his dissatisfaction with some people!! It was 12:00 a.m.… everyone in the house was sleeping that suddenly the door of Sam's room opened. When Sam opened his eyes, he saw his father who was staring at him with a sad face. Father: Sam, my son? Wake up… I need to talk to you (father and son sat in front of each other).

Sam was sad to see his father in that bad situation, but since he knew that he was emotional more than his father, he tried to calm down when his father talked! Iraj, Sam's father, had made his mind to give a negative answer to his friend next day!! However, he knew it well that all of the letters of credits would put him in jail… regardless of all different opinions he had with Sam in the family, he wanted to talk to his son about the future. He wanted to say that he father would be absent in the family! He wanted to ask everyone in the family to help each other when he was away in order to preserve the family. They talked to each other till the morning. Sam asked about the past and his father answered all of the questions enthusiastically.

The morning arrived. Sam's father took the phone and dialed his friend's number.he talked to his friend and asked him a deadline to give his money back by working but his friend hung up after threatening a lot. Sam's father hung up and went to the window facing the street. He stared at the street and the people walking on the sidewalk. At the meantime, Sam took the phone and dialed the number, which was saved in the phone!

Sam: hello? Hi. This is Sam! I want to see you.

They set an appointment at 5:00 p.m. Sam was not sad anymore. Perhaps he could not bear watching the consecutive sorrow in his family anymore. He thought: It is better to sacrifice myself than my family!

He thought that the family must not have been destroyed. He thought: perhaps my absence makes relaxation for everyone in the family.

He went to his father and leaned against his shoulder. It was the first time he was so comfortable with his father since the childhood. His eyes were teary. He wanted to cry wholeheartedly next to his father, but he went back to his room and opened the window. He took his head out of the window and shouted loudly: God!

He called God. Sam was a young man who was tired, there was no energy, whether positive or negative, inside him. He put his head on his both hands and looked at the tears dropping down. As he got calm down, he decided to sleep by 5:00 p.m. to say goodbye to this world for a few hours.

He had headache for a few days. His mood was not stable and weird behaviors had been created in him. It was 4:30 p.m. when Sam woke up and went to the kitchen. He had become a soulless body. His body was thin and weak and his face was white like the plaster on the wall. These signs showed his weak physical and mental status. His hands were shivering. He drank some water, breathed deeply, went to the hall, put on his gray jacket, and left the house. On the sidewalk, he began walking slowly. The sky was completely cloudy and dark and had formed a sad scene above his head. His legs had no power to walk. As he thought about where he was really going although he knew that he had an appointment, it was as if he had a weird fear from his future. He could not think about anything. He had made an appointment at the intersection at the neighborhood. When he thought about his father's friend, he felt distressed, his heart began beating fast, and it was as if there was nobody in this world to help him. His look was full of words and he did not know to whom he had to complain. There was neither a hand to hold his hands not a shoulder to put his head on and talk about his sorrow and feel being. Sometimes life is some scenes of a street film where pure people are its ordinary actors. Nobody ever accepts to play another role. Everyone complain about themselves and others!! This is the story of human life… being human is difficult! Sam arrived at the place. He looked at four sides of the intersection, stood there, and put his hands into his jacket pockets because of the cold weather. He looked at the people who were passing him and talked to them without saying anything. He thought that all of them were happy and the whole pain in the world just belonged to him… ! At that moment when Sam was deeply thinking about such things, an expensive car stopped in front of him. Sam went to the car, opened its door, and got in to the car. A 60-year-old man with eyes full of lies, a smile implying deception, and a disgusting look was taking then wheel. He was Mr. Yousef, the friend of Sam's father. Mr. Yousef: Hi Sam! How are you, boy?! How is your father?! Sam: Can I say something before accepting all conditions and doing my job? Mr. Yousef: yes, go on… Sam: I wanted to tell you that you are one of the parasites of this society old man! Jerk! Mr. Yousef: you are useless just like your father. You don't have even the courage to do this, did you know that Sam?

Sam: what should I do?

Mr. Yousef: Smuggling!! From one city to another! Sam: I'll do it just once. Instead, you have to return all of the letters of credit you took from my father. Now you must call my father and tell him that we are good and he can pay his debt whenever he can. Mr. Yousef accepted and they made an appointment for tomorrow morning. Sam got out of the car and doubtfully looked at Mr. Yousef who was sitting in the car. Mr. Yousef drove his car away. Sam, breathed deeply to overcome his stress. Then, he went to the house. While walking on the way home, suddenly a hand touched his shoulder gently. Sam turned around and saw his friend, Farhad, who was standing in front of him. Suddenly, his eyes got teary and he thought how calm his happy friend was standing in front of him!! But he was happy that Farhad did not have any problem of Sam in his life! It was as if Farhad had noticed many things in Sam's eyes and had realized his inner mood! Sam was a poor and hungry guy with pale face in Farhad's eyes. Farhad invited him to sit in his car and hang out together that night. Happiness could be seen in Sam's eyes. He went to the Farhad's car after him. When Farhad got in the car, he decided to do something for his friend to have fun but how?! When Sam had become a depressed man! Sam was hopeless with the world around him but was just spending his days. To him, the value of family was more than the world in his look, he was weak and had no mental focus in his life. While driving, Farhad looked at Sam and suddenly he felt scared. Perhaps his feeling was because of his friendly and brotherly feelings. Farhad: Sam?! What have you done with yourself?! Why are you like this my friend?!

Tell me if you really like to, maybe I can help! Sam told his story gradually and with a catch in his throat. He told him even about the last few seconds. Farhad was staring at Sam with a strange concern!! He stopped in front of a one of the best coffee shops in the city and asked Sam to get out and enter the coffee shop together but Sam was feeling shy of his appearance. He did not like to get out of Farhad's car. he was tired and distressed of everything. Farhad noticed it and assured Sam that they would have fun. After a few minutes, they entered the coffee shop together. Sam was looking around and a strange feeling told him: everyone is rich here. It was getting dark. Farhad's phone rang and he answered his expensive phone: Hello? Hi mom, I'll come home a bit late. Tonight, I'm out with one of my best friends! Don't worry. After his talk, Farhad put his phone on the table and began talking to Sam. Farhad told Sam that he would like to help him. Farhad's father was a retired policeman and he told Sam that he should not tell Mr. Yousef anything about this issue!! And he had to behave very normally. Farhad decided to invite Sam to his house in order to talk to his father about the problem which had happened to Sam and his family. Suddenly, Sam's face was wiped off of sadness and terror and then a beautiful smile appeared on his face, as if he had begun a new life! (Sometimes, people would like to insult the world around them while they are in trouble, but if a person responsible to humanity is found and helps them, they will certainly change and smile at the world beautifully). A young girl and boy were sittingat the table in front of them.

They were staring at Sam with a humiliating look. Sam lowered his head… but Farhad who had realized it, put his hand on Sam's shoulder and said: Look Sam! Many people put their feet in your shoes at the peak of happiness and think about you, so don't worry about the future my friend. Without a doubt, everything will be alright. Do you have a doubt Sam? In this issue?! Sam smiled and a positive hopeful feeling was formed in his mind about the future.... After talking a lot, they decided to walk for a while to change their mood. After half an hour of walking on the sidewalk, they returned to the car and got in. Sam's look at the lifestyle of Farhad had attracted Sam's attention. Farhad asked Sam to take the wheel and after 3-4 hours of driving on streets, Sam had become a professional driver because of his high intelligence!! According to the made appointment, they went to Farhad's house for dinner. Sam did not feel comfortable when he entered their house. He felt humiliation because of entering a beautiful house! But he did not feel worry due to Farhad's kindness. Sam was highly welcomed by Farhad and his family and was very happy with that. After having dinner, Sam, Farhad, and Farhad's father sat in front of each other in the hall and Sam told the whole story of his life. Farhad's father listened carefully to Sam's words with a look full of kindness. Then, Farhad's father began talking: my son, life is a scene for people walking and passing it. no man is eternal! Some people, who don't even deserve to be called as human are always asleep but when they are awake, they are blind and don't even notice that they have eyes to look and decide for making at least their own lives better!! He touched Sam's head and wished him happiness. After talking, they made an appointment to go to the police station with Farhad and his father tomorrow morning before going to Mr. Yousef in order to make a file against Mr. Yousef. So that, they could assign the rest of the affairs to the police. Sam thanked the great family of Farhad and said goodbye. Then, he went home. When he entered home, he saw his father who was standing sadly at the window of his room. Sam remembered himself and the bench in the park and a strange feeling came to him. He called his mother and told everything, good or bad, which had happened to him. His mother who was sad because of the bitter things which had happened, did not know if she could trust the new words and things or not!! She cried and Sam wiped off the tears of his mother with a napkin. His mother stood up and went to the room to tell the whole story of that day to Sam's father. The father entered the hall with a look full of doubt and stress. He told Sam: Sam?! Is what your mother says correct?! Sam: yes (And Sam began talking to his father)

Sam's father felt proud of his son at the peak of hopelessness by hearing his son's words. That night, a different atmosphere was in their house, as if they had seen a window in their lives for achieving peace and relaxation. Finally, they spent that night in happiness and peace. The morning arrived. Sam woke up with the mewing sound of Sami. They both looked at each other and Sam smiled at the sun and Sami. Suddenly, the phone rang and Sam, being half-asleep, left his room and went towards the phone: Hello? Yes… Hi. Sam. Sam: Hi dear Farhad, how are you? Farhad: thanks, please get ready, my father and I are coming to you to go to the police station! We have to report the issue to the police before 10:00 a.m., I mean before you go to Yousef. Sam: ok, I'll wait for you. Then, he went to his father to wake him up. After 20 minutes, their doorbell rang and everyone went to the police station. The police behaved very well with Sam. It was a very important file according to the police!! They formed a file and the relevant officer asked Sam to go to Yousef alone and begin cooperating with them in order to provide all of their information to the police, so that the police could identify and arrest all of the smugglers. Sam was assured that he would be supervised by the police all the time and no danger would threaten him. The officer gave his own number to Sam and asked him to provide the police with full reports via that number or refer to the police station if necessary. They said goodbye to each other. Sam had to go to Mr. Yousef at 10:00 a.m. Farhad accompanied him to near the intended intersection. After waiting for a long time, Mr. Yousef arrived and Sam opened the car door and got in the car. Sam: where are we going?

Mr. Yousef: before you do your job, we have to talk to each other with full honesty and trust. (after passing several streets and intersections, Mr. Yousef parked in front of a very expensive and extraordinary chic house1!). Before opening the house door, another car arrived. A man got out of that car and walked to the expensive car of Mr. Yousef, he asked the address of a house which was two blocks away from that big villa where he wanted to enter! Mr. Yousef looked suspiciously at the man! And gave him directions. The man went to ring the doorbell of that house and then entered it. Sam had completely realized the story! the one who had asked the address was a police officer!! Sam's face was not pale anymore and his stress was somehow mitigated. The door of the big villa was opened by a worker who was working in the villa! And Mr. Yousef's car entered the yard which was full of big trees and had a cobbled pavement. After a short walk, they approached a very big and glorious building. In in the middle of the trees in the yard, Sam noticed some guys holding guns and saying hi to Mr. Yousef from distance and he also nodded at them. At the same time, a beautiful girl with a special modesty in her eyes came towards them. After giving a short glance at Sam, she began talking to Mr. Yousef. Her name was Helena. Helena: Dad, what kind of situation is this that I can't even leave the house?! I have to go to the class! Mr. Yousef calmed her down and pointed out that they were having a guest that day! And she had to wait until the guest leaves. Sam's mind got busy thinking! Mr. Yousef who had noticed this put his hand on Sam's shoulder and accompanied him to the entrance door of the building. The maid of the house came and made way for them to enter the living room. Sam and Mr. Yousef sat in front of each other. In order to break the ice and prepare the context for their cooperation, Mr. Yousef began talking about a good life he had! But Sam had realized from the appearance of Mr. Yousef's house that who he was! And what he was doing... Sam: Can I ask a question? When we know that God has considered death for us, why should we do any piece of jerk for this short life?!

Mr. Yousef: Death is just for the people like you and your father who live in poverty under the name of reputation.

Look my son, I want to talk to you seriously. If the life of yourself and your family is important to you, you have to cooperate with me, so that nobody except me and you would know about this issue, otherwise, you know what will happen boy! Did you understand?

Sam: I understand you and people like you! Whatever you say!

Mr. Yousef: I'll return all of the letters of credit your father gave me after finishing the job. You will earn a lot with your second job!! Don't worry. You will earn a great amount of money boy. Sam: are you thinking of your daughter? What would happen to her if one day you are not here? Mr. Yousef: It's not important! Her bank account is full of money; she can be happy without me! Sam: what if someone asks her: what's your father's job? What can she say?!

Mr. Yousef looked at Sam and then remained silent.

After talking to each other, they agreed that Sam would go there again at 9:00 p.m. to talk more about the job. Sam stood up and took a pathetic look at Mr. Yousef and then left the living room and entered the yard. Suddenly, Helena appeared. She was a girl full of pride and beauty whose innocent face was shining the sun. Samhad fully realized it by looking at Helena's eyes. After taking a kind look, Sam said goodbye to her and went to the exit door. As he opened the door and turned back, he saw an innocent look behind the window. It was Helena who was looking at Sam!

Sam left the house and closed the door. He began walking on the sidewalk that suddenly he noticed that a man was walking behind him. Sam began running and entered an alley. Then, he realized that nobody was chasing him anymore. After a few seconds of pause, he entered the same street and went to his house. As he approached the house, he saw his fluffy cat Sami at the window of his room. Sami was lying down at the window, as if it wanted to tell Sam that it was alone like him! He twisted the key into the lock and entered the house. Inside the hall, he saw his father who was waiting for him. His mother smiled as she saw Sam. Sam said hi and sat in front of his father.

He told everything happened to him that day. At the same time, the phone rang. It was the police officer who began talking to Sam on the phone. The police assured Sam that the entire house and all people in the house were being monitored by the police. Also, the police officer said that he would call him in 2 hours again to remind him of the next plan. Sam said goodbye and hung up the phone. As he turned his face, he saw his father's scared and pale face who was looking at him!

His father began telling some tips of the life bitterness!! Father: Sam? Some of the things which happen in life, remind me of leaving this world with the difference that they remind me that this material world has an end. Although this world is a bit empty of spirituality, fortunately beginning the spiritual life with God will be certainly a big and new beginning. My son, I'm happy that I've been oppressed in this world because I have not oppressed anyone! Sam looked down and listened carefully to his father. A hopeful smile appeared on his lips. He went to his room and as he opened the door, he saw his lovely cat Sami that was lying at the window and watching outside. Sam touched his cat and then left it alone. He lied on his bed and closed his eyes slowly and then fell asleep. One hour passed and Sam woke up. He saw his mother standing by him. Mother: Sam? Your friend Farhad is here (Sam's mind was busy and he was staring at the ceiling with sad eyes and raised eyebrows). Sometimes, human becomes so tired of his life that he regrets the life of others and how painful it is when he cannot see the future to at least be happy with the bright future waiting for him!! Human is a creature with a modest character because he has wisdom, how funny it is that we think negatively about each other and have misconceptions. Perhaps it's my fault that I am alive?! And perhaps it's my fault that I have lost my hope and neglected God's look at me?! These were the words inside Sam's mind and heart… He was talking to the ceiling of his room! he got up, hugged Sami, put it on his desk, and talked to it. Sam: Sami? My friend, how different your life is from our colorful lives!! You are quiet but you don't deceive me with your silence. You don't bother me and return the favor with your sad look or your happiness to me, Sami! I may never return to this room again and maybe this is the last time we are sitting in front of each other and I'm talking to you and you are listening to me. Can you believe that I don't know what will happen when I leave this room?! I'm tired my friend, tired of being alone, being nothing. Sam's mother opened the door and entered the room. Mother: Sam? Someone wants to speak with you on the phone. Sam: who is it? Mother: It's a girl! Sam: Ok mom, I'm coming. Sam touched Sami's head and left the room. he went to the phone and answered the phone. Sam: hello (a girl was on the phone who was speaking fast while panting). Hello Sam. Sam: who's speaking?

The girl: I'm Helena. Mr. Yousef's daughter. I don't have enough time, Sam? Don't go to the meeting with my father. Sam: if I don't go, my family will become more miserable than before, do you understand? Helena: I promise you that nothing will happen to your family, my father is angry at you because you ratted him out... he will kill you…

Sam: how did he notice? Helena: He has seen the police! Sam: well? What should we do?! Helena: Sam! If my father leaves me, I'll get alone forever.

(Silence between their words)

Helena: Come to the bus stop in front of our house, I will sit there until you come. Goodbye. Sam hung up the phone, but the phone rang again. It was the police officer! After talking a lot, the police officer got convinced that Helena was innocent in this file! Police could enter Mr. Yousef's shelter from that moment and arrest him. Sam hung up the phone and left the house. His destination was the bus stop in front of Mr. Yousef's house. He could see Helena from distance who was sitting on an empty bench. She was putting her two hands on her cheeks and thinking deeply. Sam approached her and with a look full of doubts, to Helena and himself, sat on the same bench and stared at Mr. Yousef's house which was in front of him…The door of Mr. Yousef's house which had decorated a terrifying scene in their eyes was shining in the color of terror and black while it was white. At the meantime, something weird happened! Lots of soldiers and police officers entered Mr. Yousef's house and Sam and Helena were watching the scene in extreme shock. After a few seconds, Mr. Yousef and his comrades, while being handcuffed, were guided towards the police cars Sam and Helena were looking at the other side of the street with their wide eyes. Sam looked at Helena and noticed that she was crying for her father. Sam did not exactly know if he was asleep or awake!!

Sam: I don't know what to say?! You help me to understand this world and living in this world, I really don't understand!! Helena: don't say anything, it's useless… I'm really alone, a bad father is still a father! I don't have anybody else in this world, do you understand what I say? Sam stood up and began walking slowly on the sidewalk. A few steps away from the station, he turned around and stared at Helena whose face was full of tears. Sam returned to her again!

He looked at Helena. Sam: what will you do now? Helena: I'll talk to myself and God in a house full of loneliness. Sam smiled sadly and pointed to her to stand up and walk with him along the sidewalk. They began walking. Helena will live a life with no problem because of the wealth his father left to her but in the palace where there was no sign of life, she was really alone now. Sometimes, an early loneliness is an unbelievable nightmare to humans but how beautiful this concern of loneliness is because people get more familiar with each other at these moments when the price of kindness waves in front of peoples' eyes at all moments of life! Sam and Helena left each other and stepped towards their new lives. As Helena arrived at her house, she looked at the house and then she stood there watching the house! She was shocked. She did not know where she was going!! Then, she opened the door and stepped into the big yard. She put her hands into her pockets. After looking at the floor of the yard with her tearful eyes, she began walking in the big garden outside of the building. There was a white metal swing which had given a special view to the corner of the yard. She pushed the swing forward with her hands. Suddenly, a heavy catch in her throat and eyes pressed her whole body. She held the swing with her hands and looked at it and then reviewed the memories of her childhood. She sighed deeply and after a few moments, she saw on the swing... she began singing a children's song she sang with her father while sitting on the same swing when she was a child... she burst into tears out of loneliness. Then, she began singing while putting her hands on her face. Such tears only come from someone lonely with this level of loneliness and there is only one companion to them who is lonely too...

She stared at the sky and her tears fell down her cheeks one after another. She stood up and went to the house building. A beautiful big house which contained a world full of loneliness. Sam who was sad about Helena and could not go to his house was walking along the sidewalk. Suddenly, he stood and stared at the people walking past him and he repeated the name "Helena" several times... he was worried, so he went to the house which was familiar to him! When he arrived at the house, he paused a bit and with his sad and red eyes, he felt that he was scared for no reason! why was he so worried about someone else?! The night had arrived and the sky was terribly dark. After a few minutes that Sam rang the doorbell, he noticed that nobody was going to open the door of that house!! He was badly stressed, so he decided to climb the wall and look at the yard. He did it and realized that all of the house lights were off and Helena was in the absolute dark! Sam was worried for her mental status, so he decided to enter the house. He jumped into the yard from the top of the wall. On the cobblestone pavement of the yard, he walked towards the house building. He pressed the door handle downward and surprisingly, he noticed that the door was open!! He entered the hall in the dark and in disbelief, he saw a scene which he had never seen by far!! Helena was lying on the floor in the dark that only the light of the moon and stars had created a scary scene next to the window facing the yard. Sam put his hand on the switch to turn on the light in the hall but was scared to press it. he was scared of light at that moment!! Finally, he turned on the light and Sam saw Helena who had cut her hand and was lying in blood on the floor! Sam was shocked and could not do anything. In the big space of the house, it was only the voice of Sam that was echoed to himself!

After those terrible seconds, an ambulance stopped in front of the house and some nurses immediately transferred Helena to the ambulance. A police officer was asking questions from Sam who was shocked and very sad as if he was having a nightmare. When the policeman was asking questions, Sam suddenly felt a severe dizziness. Sam leaned against the wall and after a few seconds, he fell down. In the human world, there are two big and important points which push us forward and they are nothing but love and again love and hope in tomorrow, hope in good and romantic days to the whole creation! Looking and living, this is the wisest kind of human life which is getting destroyed gradually...

Helena had tried to kill herself out of loneliness but Sam had tried to kill himself with patience while standing.... It was after midnight. Sam was lying on a bed in one of the rooms of the hospital and a volume expander was placed into his hand. Helena was in the surgery room because of the too much wounds in her body. Outside of the room, Sam's parents were spending the moments in bitterness in the long corridor. They were very stressed and upset. The doctor came out of Sam's room and looked at Sam's parents, implying that Sam had no special problem. Sam's parents got calm a bit and his father went to the yard of the hospital to have some privacy. With all that stress, he was hopeful to end that night well!

He began walking. His steps were slow, heavy, and manly. As he arrived at the security room of the hospital, suddenly he saw his reflection in the glass door of the security room! he paused a bit and was shocked. Worry was obvious in his face but he had cried deeply inside he thought: how quick the youth ends! Some pictures of himself at the age of 23 emerged in fort of his eyes and his eyes got teary. He raised his head and took a hopeful look at God who was looking at him from the sky. Meanwhile, suddenly he heard the shouts of her wife thanking God. It showed that Sam had got back to normal state. Sam's parents went towards Sam's room and stood by his bed. Sam looked at his parents with his half opened eyes and as he saw his father, he got sad about him! He saw his mother whose face was white like the plaster on the wall. Father: How are you dear? Are you ok?! Sam: I'm fine dad, can't be better than this! Dad? How is Helena? Father: good, she's passed the danger. If you are ok, she's ok too! (4:00 a.m.). Sam's mother had put her head on her two hands and had fallen asleep by his son's bed. Sam opened his eyes and looked around at his mother who was holding his hand. He breathed deeply and closed his eyes. He was thinking about Helena who was taking rest two rooms farther… he separated his mother's hand offhis hand very gently and came out of the bed quietly. He held the volume expander bar in his hand and left the room. He walked slowly and quietly in the corridor until he reached Helena's room. he went into the room and stood by her. After a few minutes of staring at her with his patient and tired eyes, he called her several times: (Helena? Helena?! Are you awake?). He felt a strange sorrow in his chest, as if he was talking to himself slowly! He looked at the window facing the yard of the hospital. In the darkness, he went towards the window, stood in front of it, and stared out of the window. His tears fell on his cheeks, as if he did not like to wipe his tears off his face!! He loved his tears patiently… those tears were the soundless companions of Sam… he thought: how beautiful are the stars shining in the sky, but what a pity none of them belongs to me or… He looked at Helena and continued: Helena…! He turned to the window and began murmuring romantic words. The clock hands passed each other and Sam was still standing by the window. He did not notice the passing of time anymore... Sam and Helena got discharged after a few days. Sam returned to his house and as he opened the door of his room, he saw Sami that was lying at the window. It was as if Sami was taking its last breathes, as it was yawning, Sami touched its head. Those hands were familiar to Sami. It turned around and sat in front of Sam. With its quiet and sad meowing, as if it was talking to Sam. They were both leaning against the window and staring out of the window. Sam: you're my only friend Sami, you don't know anything about my loneliness in this weird world! Honestly, I am tired, I wish were not living in this world Sami, I don't understand this world. where is our place in this world?! As Sam told the unsaid words inside his hear to Sami, drops of tears appeared on Sami's cheeks. Sam looked at Sami and then at the window and street. Then, he went to his bed, lied on it, and fell asleep due to severe tiredness. (8:30 p.m.). Sam's eyes were opening slowly and his mind got more conscious. He saw his mother standing by him. Mother: Sam? My son?! I tried hard to wake you up at noon but you didn't, get up my son, dinner is ready! Sam: ok, I'll come. Mother left the room and closed the door. Sam sat on his bed and turned his head to the window. He saw Sami, his fluffy and sad cat, that was lying down suspiciously without moving and had put its head at one side. Sam called Sami twice but Sami did not move!! Sam stood up and went to the window, touched Sami's head, but it did not breathe. Sam: Sami? My friend? You… you are going too?! Sleep my friend, be relax. Sam's eyes got full of tears. Suddenly, his mother knocked at the door.

Mother: Sam? Dinner is getting cold sweetie.

Sam: I don't feel like eating now. Mother: (after a pause): Ok dear…

Sam's body began shivering slightly and he felt a severe fever. He went to the heater in his room, turned it up, but he had forgotten that the heater did not work properly when its flame was up. He went to his bed and closed his eyes, then he fell asleep very soon because of too much dizziness.

(3:00 a.m.). The heater candle did not work properly and was put in the state of gas leakage!! The room got polluted gradually. Sami was lying at the window and Sam was hallucinating at sleep. He had too much fever and because of the breathing problem which had occurred to him, he took his last breaths and died…

Next to Sami's body, Sam's soul stood and touched Sami's head! The door was opened and Sam's mother took a look at the dead body of Sami and then went to Sam's bed!! He was staring at the dead body of her son. Nurses and police officers were passing Sam's soul that was standing at the door without seeing him…. Sam's family was crying but Sam was staring at his dead body and also Sami! He was looking at them with astonishment!!

It is true that human is the supreme creature but sometimes, some people want to see each other miserable which shows the very small and ugly worldview of such people, just like Mr. Yousef who was so selfish that even the destiny of Sam's family was not important to him… of course, such people will face a punishment by God after their death.

Sam could be analogized to a fragrant flower in spring that grew in spring but was decayed in fall and winter.

His family was deeply and highly stressed. They could not understand what had happened!! Sam was looking at his mother innocently when she passed him crying. Sam's soul went to the window of his room of loneliness, he looked at the window and street, and then looked at the park where a bench was the companion of his lonely days. Then, he went to his dead body slowly, stood there, and stared at his dead body. After a few seconds, he got out of his mundane room…

While getting out of the room, he saw Farhad who was entering his room so sadly. Farhad was sitting at Sam's bed and staring at his dead body. He remembered some memories. Farhad was very shocked by watching the death of his only friend who was asleep forever…

The emergency nurse put his head on Farhad's shoulder and told him that the corpse had to be transferred to the hospital morgue. Farhad went to the window and stared out of the window. Perhaps he could not believe that his friend, Sam, had left him forever?! And he could not be alive anymore in this world… Farhad went to his father's car and they drove to their house. As they arrived at the house, Farhad's father (Mr. Ghasem Abadi) parked the car in front of the house door and then got out!

He hit the car alarm but as he turned his head around, he noticed that Farhad did not get out of the car but was staring at the end of the street. A weird sadness was seen in his look. His father knew that he had to leave Farhad alone for a few minutes to calm down. He undid the car alarm to the opened door state, took the house key out of his pocket, opened the door, and temporarily ran from the sad loneliness of Farhad. Perhaps we cannot realize the presence of someone we know in this big world until we lose them!! and that moment is the most difficult sadness for we, lonely humans, which will occur in our hearts. Perhaps, Farhad had not seen Sam as he had to see his friend. He could never imagine him as dead!...

Chapter Two

It was 3:00 a.m. and Farhad was deeply asleep on the back seat of the car. at the meantime, suddenly a hand hit the car window and woke him up. Mr. Ghasem Abadi, Farhad's father, asked him to go into the house. He accompanied Farhad to his room and asked him to be relax as time will solve everything… Farhad's father turned off the light and left the room. Farhad had put his hands on his sad face, yawned, and then looked at the walls of his room in absolute darkness. The sadness of losing his friend appeared in his tired eyes, but he was tired, tired, tired of everything… he closed his eyes and fell asleep. (8:00 a.m. in front of the morgue). Everyone was waiting for the ambulance. Farhad was staring at Sam's family members who were crying. He did not know why he could not breathe. He was shocked and his tears could not fall. He had not believe that he was not going to see his friend Sam anymore!! He was struggling with doubt and certainty. Ambulance had arrived. Farhad was deeply stuck in his thoughts that he had not noticed the ambulance. Everyone was around the ambulance and after a few moments, the dead body of Sam was transferred to the morgue. It was time for burying Sam… all family members and relatives of Sam had stood around the grave which had become empty for Sam. Suddenly, Farhad left the crowd, went to Sam's corpse, sat there, stared at his friend and looked at him. The catch in his throat burst and he began talking to the dead body! Farhad: Sam?? My friend, how soon you left us… why?! Two people helped Farhad to stand up. After a few minutes, they put the dead body of Farhad into the grave, then they began pouring soil on him. Human comes from soil and he will return to it too… Sad moments passed after one another and everyone began leaving there but Farhad was sitting alone at the grave of his friend. He put his hand on the soil and stared at the name of Sam which was written on a paper and put on a piece of wood temporarily until the tombstone would get ready. He was looking at the grave in too much shock. A sad and bitter look. Farhad: Sam?! Bro, how lonely I am now… May God be with you my friend….

It was 5:00 p.m. and getting dark slowly.

Farhad had returned to his house. He had just lied on his bed to take some rest.

Farhad's mother (Mrs. Zeinab) entered his room, sat at his bed, and began talking to her son: May God give keep you in health sweetie. You will get old one day and this is a law in the nature of creation. Farhad: mom? I can't believe that I cannot see Sam again. Mother: I understand. It happened to my older brother when he was very young and I could not see him anymore. But darling, I just trusted in God… come on, wash your face and come to the living room, your poor dad is so sad. Farhad: ok… In a few minutes, Farhad talked to his father. Farhad's father had become more succulent than before. Farhad decided to go out for a walk. He did his clothes and hair and on the sidewalk, as he was putting his hands in the pockets of his pants, he took steps slowly. Moments passed after another and suddenly he remembered Helena!! He decided to go to her house, so he changed his way towards her house. When he arrived at her house door, he paused a bit, then he thought: what am I doing here?! I lowered his heard and thought for a while! Then, he put his hand on the door bell and pressed it for 2-3 times. Helena was sitting in a chair next to the fireplace. As she heard the doorbell, she took the door phone to see who was at the door? She saw Farhad with a very sad face! Helena felt a catch in her throat (since Farhad was the only friend of Sam…!!!) Helena: Hello Farhad. Farhad: hi, sorry for bothering but… but!? You know Sam? Sam is dead? (The sound of Helena crying was heard on the street, she was crying, whining, and sighing about Sam's fate…) What a sad whine! Farhad: Please open the door, I have just a few questions about Sam, maybe they're very important points about Sam that just you know. I want to know them all. Helena: ok, ok… Farhad entered the house and after saying hi to each other, they sat on the sofa in the living room in front of each other. Their eyes were red. Helena: Farhad, what happened to Sam… tell me what happened? What exactly do you want to know about him? Why are you here to ask about Sam? Where were you before Farhad… ?!

Farhad: I don't know what to say Helena?! Will you tell me the truth if I ask a question? Helena: ask, Farhad: did you… did you really love Sam?! Helena was staring at Farhad while frowning and crying. She put her hands on her face and began whining sadly!! Farhad went to the window and looked outside when he was feeling a bitter catch in his throat. After a few seconds, he went to the yard and then to the exit door. Then, he left the house and began walking in the avenue. He was walking along the avenue slowly. Farhad could not focus on his thoughts, he was walking slowly and quietly… Minutes passed but Farhad was only looking at the people passing him in hurry. He doubted if they had really no problem?! If they had no problem, why were they so happy? Farhad, as if he was a human with no pain, was in a stormy sea which had drowned him like others. When he arrived at the house door, he took his keys out of his pocket and opened the door. When he entered the house, he looked at his parents sadly and then went to the room of his loneliness… what is Farhad's pain?! He took some rest, put his hand on his forehead, closed his eyes, stared at the ceiling, and suddenly remembered his friend Sam. He reviewed all of the seconds in his mind, got up, went to the window, opened it, and stared at the park in front of their house. He remembered Sam who said once the park and a bench in it were his only friends…. He did not notice when his mother (Mrs. Zeinab) opened the door of his room and looked at her son in that bitter situation!... Drops of tears fell down his mother's eyes. She leaned her head against the door and was only sad about her son. Farhad's father was standing in the living room and thinking about his wife and son who were sad and distressed. He felt a weird catch in his throat and was still looking at them. Farhad: Mom, please leave me alone. Mother (after a short pause!!) left the room and closed the door. Helena was like a captive in a house which was a friend of silence. Farhad took the phone and dialed her number. Helena: Hello? Farhad: hi, are you ok? Helena: thanks, I'm fine… Farhad: Helena, I wanted to discuss something with you, of course I know that you are not in a good condition to talk about these things but it would be good for both of us to talk now. Helena: I'm listening. Farhad: I've decided to marry you if you want? (Helena was silent on the phone meaningfully!!). Farhad: Helena? We both lost a mutual friend, the best thing to be with each other is marrying! I am sad because of Sam's death, so are you! You are alone and so am I… just like Sam who is alone!! We can be together forever. Helena:

Farhad, I want some time to think, will you wait? Farhad: yeah, as long as you want… Farhad was thinking while holding the phone in his hand… after they finished talking, Farhad went to his room, looked at the walls of his room, sighed deeply, lied on his bed, closed his eyes, and fell asleep out of tiredness! His room was full of cliché and sorrow and he was not laughing in his room anymore!! Farhad who was an only child had got more involved in the sorrow of his loneliness… he had no choice but putting up with the conditions. His mother had wanted to clean up his room but he asked his mother to let him do that. All of these changes were because Farhad loved being lonely but he was unaware of the fact that he was captured by loneliness! He had used to it and did not exchange it with anything else. He had communicated with loneliness intimately and all walls in his room were full of old pieces of newspaper he had once a fan of. He had also written some beautiful poems with black pencil.

Night had arrived and Farhad was struggling with a horrible nightmare in sleep that suddenly the phone ringing startled him up. He got up and went to the phone. Farhad: Hello? Helena: Hi!! Farhad: Hi… Helena: come to the bus stop in front of our house in 1 hour, I will be waiting for you there.

Farhad: Ok, I'll come… !! Farhad hung up the phone, stood in front of the mirror, did his messy hair with his hands and opened the door of his room and then left the house. He was walking slowly towards the same bus stop and thinking: If Helena says no, is there any other reason to convince her that I really love her? No..! Moments passed one after another and Farhad was still walking on the sidewalk. After 1 hour, Farhad arrived at the bus stop. He saw Helena who was sitting alone on the bench. He approached her and stood in front of her. They both looked at each other with their tired eyes. Farhad: Hi Helena… Helena: Sit down... Farhad sat on the bench of Helena's loneliness! They stared at the street ground for a few seconds with their sleepy, tired, and sad eyes… (Helena looked at Farhad) and then she looked at the street with her sad eyes while touching her fingers and thinking deeply… Helena: Farhad?! Exactly the same spot we are sitting and the spot you are sitting now, someone was sitting two days ago and talking to me to take away my loneliness… (Helena began crying) but now he is not here anymore… I don't know when I'm going to meet him?!! You claim that you are his friend (Farhad's eyes got tearful as he heard Helena's words as he was still staring straight ahead). Helena: if you are his real friend, I trust you and am ready to marry you!! But there is a problem, your father is a retired colonel! How can he accept that his son marries the daughter of a smuggler?!! (Farhad had stared at Helena for a few moments) Farhad: You answered your question, what's your fault if your father is a smuggler? Farhad leaned back and breathed a sigh of relief. His face was a bit happy now. Sometimes, they looked at each other politely and smiled, as if they had found a strange and inner medicine for the pain of being lonely and that medicine was called love which had made them so much happy.

They both stood up and after saying goodbye to each other, each one went towards his house. Helena stood in front of her house door and in absolute loneliness, as if all of the sorrows had collapsed again on her head, did not want to bear loneliness even for one second. She twisted the key in the lock, opened the door, and walked among the trees in the yard. She arrived at the building, opened the door, entered the building, and then closed the door. She stood there at the door and leaned against it. the catch in her throat burst slowly and began crying. The only sound which was echoed to herself was her sound of whining… the night passed with all of its loneliness for Farhad and Helena and another morning was coming. (9:30 a.m.). Farhad's eyes opened slowly and a sound had made him wake up. He saw his mother standing by him and staring at him! She had a beautiful smile on her face. Mother: Come to the kitchen honey, your breakfast is ready. Farhad: ok mom. Then, his mother went to the door to get out of the room. Farhad: mom? Don't go please, I have a word with you. Mother: tell me darling, I'm listening! Farhad: Mom! I… I have decided to marry… Mother: tell me who is that lucky girl?!

Farhad said nothing. but after a few minutes, he continued: Helena!! Mother: The same girl Sam loved?!

Farhad: Yes, mom…

Mother: Do you know that her father… ?!

Farhad: Mom, I love her, do you understand? Mother: It's ok with me but what about your father? He will certainly disagree. Farhad: Then, I'll do what I should not. Mother: what sweetie? Farhad: I'll leave this house; I'll go somewhere to live in peace. Mother: Please don't say that again, everything will be alright, maybe your father agrees and maybe not! Let's have breakfast and then I'll talk with your father. Farhad: ok, let's go... There was lots of bread, dairy products, and juice on the table. Farhad had just started eating breakfast that the phone rang. Farhad stopped eating and went to the phone. Helena was on the other side of the phone line. Farhad picked the phone and began talking. Farhad: Hello? Helena: Hi Farhad. Farhad: Are you ok?? After talking, they said goodbye to each other and Farhad returned to the table. Mother: honey, to whom were you talking? Farhad: You know that, why do you ask?

Mother: Farhad! This relationship is a mistake because your father must have certainly an opinion on this special case. Farhad: I don't want to hear; do you understand mom? His mother's eyes got red as if her heart was broken. She was staring at Farhad. Farhad stood up and left the kitchen. He had frowned and his mind did not want to think about anything. He left the house and went to the park in front of their house. As he entered the park, he sat on a bench which was surrounded by green trees. As he was looking at the children playing in the park, he remembered his friend Sam. The day they were both sitting on the same bench and talking to each other. Sometimes we cannot trust in life, so that you get unaware of your tomorrow despite the whole knowledge in the world. there, you remember God in your heart.

Farhad stood up and walked on the cobblestone pavement in the park. After walking for a while, he went back to the same bench and stared at the same children who were playing happily. He was worried about the next day that he did not know anything about the destiny. He stood up and went to the house. He saw his father who was talking to mother. He remained silent to understand their words about him, but he just heard one sentence of his father: The hell my son will to marry that girl!!!! He was looking at the pale wall in front of him.

He had put his forehead on his weak wrist. He passed his parents just like a black shadow and went to the room of his loneliness. When he entered the house, he closed the door and stood behind it. he was feeling frustrated. Farhad did not want to disrespect his parents. That is why he avoided arguing with them. he heard his father again who said: That's my word!! Farhad lied on his bed, closed his eyes, and fell asleep.

Sometimes in a warm room which is not cold like the cold weather outside in winter, cold thoughts overcome us as if we are spending the time in the middle of a cold and empty cemetery.

On the four steps at the entrance of the house in front of which there was a beautiful garden, Helena, the beautiful girl who was struggling with the sorrow of her loneliness, was sitting and staring at the sky which had brought the beautiful winter sunlight for her tired body and mind. She had put her right hand under her chin and with her eyes full of wish was demanding the sky to sympathize with her and not withhold the beautiful winter sunlight! Making love with the sky was so pure that drowned human in the philosophy of God greatness… Maybe the creator of Earth and heavens gives a positive answer to all of this beautiful and inner praying. Human is not afraid of being alone when the sky becomes his companion and talks to him. The trees empty of leaves and full silence had made a pleasant winter space in Helena's eyes and heart. Sometimes she used the painting stuff she had because of her talent and interest in painting since the childhood to keep her inner relaxation and paint the sky and garden in the house. When she began painting, she felt relaxed and the whole sorrow in her heart was thrown away. While painting, a cold wind blew into the house through the window. She felt cold, wrapped her shawl around herself, and began painting again. After a few hours, she finished painting and wrote at the bottom of the painting: Dedicated to all moments of my loneliness… she stared at her beautiful painting and after a small pause, she went to the window, looked at the sky and noticed that the winter sunlight was shining in the half cloudy sky while snowflakes were falling down in a scattered way. her red and teary eyes had become full of happiness.

It was full of gloom… full of contemplation… that sometimes we love experiencing one moment of others' lives… shame on me! And people like me!! (me and those who are asleep…) Helena went to the phone and decided to talk to Farhad about the beautiful thing which had happened in the house and her painting! At the meantime, the phone rang. She picked the phone: Hello?

It was aunt Shamsi on the other side of the line. She had been living in America for 20 years. Aunt Shamsi: hi sweetie, how are you?! Helena: I'm fine auntie, what happened that you remembered your niece? Aunt Shamsi: what are you talking about? I'm your aunt…

Helena: You have never called my father even once in these 20 years. My father always said that he had forgotten that he had a sister! How did you remember that I would be alive?! Aunt Shamsi: Honey, you have to listen to me, your father had become a dangerous criminal who was running the life of people around him, he didn't take our advice seriously. He didn't even think that you, his daughter, would realize his job one day, that's why the relationship between me and your father was meaningless, my love, please believe me. Helena: Aha, you are right…! Aunt Shamsi: Helena? You are alone now, my son is also grown up and is ready to marry, it will be very nice if you come here to marry my son!! You cannot live alone forever, can you? Helena: I'm sorry auntie, I love a boy here and we are going to marry! Helena and her aunt said goodbye to each other after talking a lot. As Helena hung up the phone, it rang again. Helena: Hello? Farhad: Hi Helen, how are you? Helena: I'm fine. Farhad: We have to talk about an important issue. Helena: I'm listening, tell me. Farhad (after some pause and silence): We cannot marry, I mean we can but there is a big barrier ahead of us and that's my father. He says that he will not accept me as his son if we marry and things like that! But believe me Helena, I really love you… and there is nobody like you for me in this world … I'm telling the truth Helena… Farhad was talking that Helena hung up without saying goodbye! The burden of losing her father and Sam had made her life bitter and Farhad's behavior was also throwing a new sadness to her pains. She sat on the floor and put her forehead gently on her both hands. She thought about the temporary happiness of one hour ago and also about the beautiful paining. She was giving her bitter laugh with shivering tears to the sky. Days passed and Helena did not know that these moments were the moments of her life passing one after another. She was scared of the future and did not know what would happen?! Just like all other humans!...

A miss is as good as a mile; life had brought a nightmare full of loneliness to her that she was just spending her days… Farhad who had realized that Helena was upset with his words made a big decision!! Farhad decided to just call her for a month and avoid going to her house, so that Helena would calm down. He decided to convince her via the phone that he really loved her… cold days and night were passing one after another for Farhad in loneliness and sorrow! None of his calls was answered! Nobody answered the sad Farhad… he was going to believe that he had no place in Helena's heart until that he thought maybe Helena had never understood his inner feeling?! He counted the days until he decided to go to her. He did his messy hair in front of the mirror in his room, put on his clothes, and left the house. He began walking on the sidewalk until he arrived at Helena's house. He rang the doorbell several times but nobody answered. He was waiting to hear Helena's voice any minute but he just heard the sound of the doorbell. He thought: she's very angry with me! So I'll sit here until she answers!! After a few moments, a big man who was carrying some boxed arrived at the house door and looked at Farhad in wonder in wonder. The big man: hey, what do you want here? Whom do you want to see? Farhad: Can I ask you what you are doing here? The big man: I've rented this house for a week, to whom do you want to talk? Maybe I can help you?! Farhad stood up and began talking. Farhad: Can you tell me where the owner of this house is? The big man: I don't know, I just gave her the money and rented the house. That's it boy… (Farhad was more disappointed than ever. He sat on the ground in front of the house, put his hands on his forehead, and stared at the ground). The big man nodded and while looking at Farhad with his eyes indicating sympathy, entered the house and closed the door…

Farhad had become a professional night watchman! Sometimes, he did not go home at nights. His hair had grown and his body was full of lice since he just took shower once a month!! Lice were in all his body and head. His clothes were stinking so badly that everyone passing him noticed!! When he entered the house in the middle of the day, his mother got worried and her eyes got full of tears as she saw her son with that worrying appearance. Farhad's situation got more terrible every day and he did not like to talk to anybody. He did not pay attention to anything, just like a partridge putting its head under the snow!

He had forgotten himself. His days had become gray and his nights were black.

(6:00 a.m.) Mr. Ghasem Abadi, Farhad's father, was standing in Farhad's room, looking at the tired body of his son who was lying on bed. Farhad's situation indicated his breakdown and the sad face of his father showed that he knew his son would not have a good fate in this life and Farhad had to pull himself together. Hehad to stop this negligence. His father did not like to wake his son up. he stood in front of the window in Farhad's room for 3-4 hours and walked in his room. he did not want to believe that if he, as a father, did not break his son's heart, his son would have never fallen in this condition.

9:00 a.m. Farhad opens and closes his eyes and gradually wakes up. A half-asleep voice drew his attention!! Farhad?? Farhad? Are you awake? Farhad looked at his father who was sitting on a chair and staring at him. The eyes of both of them were puffy and they tried not to pretend. Father: Farhad? Are you ok my son? (Farhad rubs his eyes with his hand, turns his face towards the wall, and stares at the walls). Father: I'm your father! Tell me what did I do? what kind of sin did I commit that I have to see my son like this? Talk to me my dear, tell me what's your problem? (Farhad closes his eyes and begins talking with his tired voice) Farhad: Dad, will you lit up a cigarette for me? (Mr. Ghasem Abadi's eyes get full of tears and blood and his tears fall down his male cheeks). He lowered his head and after a few moments, he began talking.

Father: I'll do that my dear, I even want to be your cigarette, be burnt, and say nothing... just know this my son that I'm ready to sacrifice myself for you to feel well! Trust me for the first and last time... (Father leaves the room and after a few minutes, he returns with a tray of full breakfast. He asks Farhad to wash his face and hands and have the breakfast his father has prepared.) A breakfast with the father and his son...!! A breakfast which was sad inside!) The father was feeling sad but he did not show his sadness. He felt that his son had a severe sorrow but he could not do anything. He swallowed the bites of catch and sadness one after another and apparently he wanted to show his son what a beautiful morning it was... ! what a weird sense of happiness has been created in us!! The talk began and the father and his son talked a lot... they got it off their chests, from yesterday until today ... (We humans are so badly involved in our routine lives that sometimes we do not even get shocked by hearing the news of each other's death and this makes us say the most bitter and difficult words in our minds: whoever dies is relieved! Good for them...!! Mrs. Zeinab (Farhad's mother) entered the room and looked at her husband and son who were talking to each other. She saw Farhad's face full of happiness, as if he had forgotten everything!! His face was succulent and happy but she noticed that her husband was so sad! Mrs. Zeinab: I've got some good news; it makes you very happy. Last night when I was at the mourning gathering of the our neighbor, I found a very good girl for our very good son, how polite and great that girl was, just like a bunch of flowers… Farhad: mom, I need one year to get prepared for marrying. That's my condition! Deal?? Mrs. Zeinab: I don't understand what you do! ok, do whatever you like… The sunset was approaching. Farhad felt like going to a happy public place to laugh and be happy as much as he could. He put on his clothes and went to the exit door of the house. Mother: Where are you going honey? Farhad: I'm going to have some fun in the amusement park!! Mother: Amusement park! Are you a kid? Farhad: yea, I think I was born again, let me have this feeling at least right now, I love this feeling very much mom…

I'm leaving, I'll be back late at night, don't worry about me. Mother: Ok! After entering the amusement park, he walked a bit and looked at different games there and then got into the fanfare. When he sat in the cabin and it began twirling and reached to the sky, he felt a weird relaxation. He looked outside of the cabin and thought: (Farhad: why are all of these people together and I am alone?!). The cabin reached the ground and Farhad began walking. He saw a booth where they sold perfume and watch. The watches were shining in Farhad's eyes. He approached the watches and asked the salesman the price of watches one after another. The salesman was a good-looking young man who had a warm voice and answered the questions of his customers with too much patience. Farhad welcomed the good behavior of the young salesman and bought a watch according to his taste.

Chapter Three

The salesman introduced himself as Amir Ali. When they began talking, Amir Ali, just like Farhad who was a new friend of him, revealed the secret of a wound in his heart. They noticed that they had something in common. That night, they walked together and got their words off their chests. This was the beginning of their friendship. In this friendship, relaxation and chivalry were holding their hands. Since then, Farhad went to Amir Ali to help him and worked with his friend. Farhad who had to join the military service and had not used the benefits of his father's job who was a retired colonel, decided to leave the city and join the military service to spend some time there. The last nights before joining the military service, he spent his time with his friend Amir Ali. Farhad was sent off to the military service and abundant changes had overcome his new character there. There were lots of men with independent characters there… but Farhad who had learned all of his positive and negative personality traits there, had different characters inside him after the end of his military service!! Unfortunately, this problem was because he got influenced very soon! He had a desire to quarrel with everyone…

Amir Ali was also unaware of his friend Farhad for two years until Farhad met. Farhad told the story of the past two years to Amir Ali and he also sympathized with Farhad and confirmed his words… that night, they began walking on the sidewalk of the street together and talked to each other. Life is always flowing. It is with us whether we want it or not, because life is flowing in our souls… nights and days passed after another and Amir Ali and Farhad had found more sense of friendship and brotherhood to each other. After two months, Farhad disappeared again! This time, a few months passed. After 6 months, Amir Ali decided to go meet Farhad and also complain a bit!! When he approached Farhad's house, it was as if he had missed his friend after 6 months. His steps had become faster. As he reached the house door, he pressed the doorbell. A kind but face-paled mother opened the door. Amir Ali realized that she was Farhad's mother. Mrs. Zeinab: Yes, my son?! How can I help you? Amir Ali: Hi, can you ask Mr. Farhad to come to the door please? I'm Amir Ali, his friend. Mrs. Zeinab: go to the third floor my son, his room is there. My son is depressed maybe you can help him and cheer him up. Amir Ali: yes, ok…! Amir Ali entered the house and then entered Farhad's room. he saw that Farhad was sitting in the corner of the room while wearing black clothes. He had put his hand on his head and had created a sad moment for himself! He was living his life like that! As Farhad raised his head and noticed the presence of Amir Ali, he stood up and stared at him. After a few seconds, tears fell down his shivering cheeks, indicating a very heavy catch in his throat. Farhad: Amir Ali? My friend… My father died of stroke, I've been here in this room for 6 months because of the sorrow of losing my father, I'm fed up, I'm dying. The sound of Farhad's crying depicted a sad image in Amir Ali's mind. Amir Ali: my friend! Some wounds cannot be treated and also cannot heal… you just have to wash them by crying…Farhad: yesterday, when I got out of the room, unfortunately I faced a problem! They sent me to the police station!! Well, they found that I was the son of Colonel Ghasem Abadi and they helped me a lot to solve my problem and freed me. Amir Ali:

what kind of problem? Farhad: Since the funeral of my father, I preferred to stay in my room for a while, I mean I couldn't go out!! Until yesterday afternoon when I decided to go for a short walk in the street. When I was walking on the sidewalk, suddenly a man came to me and slapped me on my face!! I don't know what a feeling I had but after one minute, the man realized that he had confused me with someone else!! And I was not the person he had to slap!! I had imprisoned myself in the house for several months after the funeral of my father. When I got out of the house, I wanted to change my moon but when someone slapped me hard by mistake, I slapped him too and that he had sued against me!! you see Amir Ali? How good the house is because outside, they slap you suddenly for no reason, my father is really relieved... Amir Ali: my friend, let this world continue like this!! (How beautiful it is when two lonely humans find each other and this common issue makes them respect each other more...). They decided to go to the amusement park and have a short trip. They got into the fanfare and when it began twirling slowly around itself and reached to the sky, Farhad looked at his friend Amir Ali whose eyes were sad and red and staring at his friend. Farhad: what's up? Amir Ali: nothing, I was thinking about the day when all of these people have to leave this world, I'm scared of dying... I hate leaving!! Farhad: Amir Ali? Now that you are my friend, I want you not to be scared of anything neither in this world nor the other world ok? Be strong forever... Amir Ali: ok, my friend, whatever you say. I'll not be afraid of anything from now, I promise. You know Farhad, now that we are up here and far from the chaos on the ground, I have an inner peace. I remember this beautiful sentence I read in a newspaper: Now, everything is closed!! You know?! sometimes you must write it on a piece of paper and stick it at the glass of your thoughts: It's closed! You must let your mind take some rest, put your hands under your head, stare at the sky, and whistle when your mind is free from the world. you must laugh at all of the thoughts which are in line on the other side of the glass of your mind. Then you must tell yourself: let them wait!! Amir Ali: Where are you Farhad? Farhad was sitting on the seat in the cabin of fanfare and was staring out of the cabin window!! He was drowned in his thoughts. Amir Ali: good for you Farhad, but I am in this cabin and although we are far from the ground, I am still struggling with some problems which were created by humans. I wish we were so good to be angels and never stepped on Earth. Farhad: yeah, we have to go back to Earth now... !! They both laughed at the same time!

Chapter Four

How we human beings depend part of Earth but aware unaware that the entire earth is the right of a wonderful creature called human… while talking and laughing, suddenly Amir Ali's phone rang. Amir Ali: yes (His mother was on the other side) Suddenly, Amir's face got blushed. Both his face and his eyes. He hung up the phone. Farhad: what's wrong Amir Ali? Amir: my father is not well; they took him to the hospital. I have to go. Farhad: I'll come too. Amir: No, you go home, I'll call you tomorrow. Amir Ali rushed towards the hospital to get there as soon as possible. When he entered the corridor of the hospital, he saw his mother who came to him while crying. She cried: My son, you father just died… Amir was in a weird shock, he had a catch in his throat and could not even cry. Everyone from their relatives who came to the hospital and knew about what had happened got sad but not like Amir Ali and his mother… (everyone just knows the pain of losing their fathers)… The bitterness of this world lies in its reality… now, Amir Ali was stuck under sorrows!! It was as if it was not going to end. He did not get out of the house for 40 days. After 40 days, he decided to go for a walk outside and meet his friend Farhad. When he wanted to cross the street, the traffic light turned green. Amir Ali who was not feeling well yet was walking while looking downside and he did not notice the car who was passing the green light!! He was badly shattered inside, at the meantime, the driver of the passing car shouted and insulted him. The driver: where's your father to teach you when the light is green, you have to stop for the cars to pass…what are you doing? (Amir Ali who was still sad for losing his father realized his words and a devastating sorrow came to his heart…! The world has no solution itself but fortunately, the roadmap is just in the hands of God to s how us the path…). Life is like a hand writing on a crumpled paper! We have to just take that paper and write on it again: this was life, whether good or bad…!! He returned home while being very sad. He was taking rest that the doorbell rang. Farhad entered the house and went straight to Amir Ali's room. as he opened the door of his room, he saw that the sad and crying Amir Ali was sitting in a dim corner of the room. Farhad: my friend, never be sad for the humans in this world because controlling them is not in our hands, it's in God's hands… these people have a world as big as the clothes they wear!! Of course, clothes are unaware of the inner side of humans and their worlds!

Some humans are dumb who just pretend to be dumb because others are not important to them!! you want to swim opposite to this river! You get crushed and nothing will remain from you. So just live the life you prefer because this life will continue also after you… days and months passed and Amir Ali was feeling better but his mother who, in absolute loneliness, had to tolerate the pain of losing her husband and the pain of seeing her son sad was feeling unwell. She saw the doctor and found that she had nervous diabetes. Amir Ali was feeling well but by hearing this painful news, his heart broke again and he felt sad. He was calming his mother down with a pleasant but sad smile on his face. Since he knew his mother, he was sure that she would overcome her disease. Amir decided to meet his friend Farhad to tell him what had happened. Amir and Farhad went to the cemetery where Sam was buried. They wanted to talk to their friend

Sam. Amir who had heard the story of Sam from Farhad said nothing and just followed Farhad to the cemetery. When they arrived at the cemetery and grave of Sam, they both looked at the graved photo of Sam on his gravestone and then prayed for him. Meanwhile, Amir Ali went towards the water tap to fill a container with water and wash the gravestone. Suddenly, he hit a young girl who was accompanied by a young and angry man whose face was tanned. Amir Ali began apologizing that the man suddenly began beating him so badly!! Amir tried to defend himself since he was scared to be hurt again but that man tied the fate of Amir Ali and Sam together… the angry man took a sharp knife out of his pocket and hit Amir Ali's heart. Amir fell down in blood and rolled down. Farhad who had just come to Amir heard the last sentence of Amir: Farhad? Take me to Sam's grave please… the wounded and tired body of Amir Ali who had turned into a bloody corpse was placed on Sam's grave. Farhad was looking at Amir with his wide open eyes and a terrible catch in his throat! It was as if the same scene which had happened to Farhad in Sam's room was not depicted for Farhad. A scene full of sorrow and terror! For a friend who was bearing this sad burden on his shoulder…

No word can be found for describing the mood of the character of the story (Farhd!).

Farhad was having a weird feeling just like children whose face is bit changed when they want to cry but have no tears… he was stuck in an unbelievable shock. He could not believe that Amir Ali was lying down next to Sam's grave! This is a story which cannot be written by its author… the police car siren was heard and the ambulance car had come to the scene. The murdered had escaped. The emergency doctor confirmed Amir Ali's death. Farhad was staring at the dead body of Amir that was transferred by the ambulance. This story of loneliness is very long! It had been transferred to Farhad to be really alone after Sam's death…! Farhad was feeling sad. He preferred to walk from the cemetery to his house. He had the same painful feeling that he had after Sam's death. when he arrived at home, his mother opened the door and as she saw Farhad so paled and sad, she wanted to know more why his son was so distressed? She was worried about Farhad and was wondering what happened to him.

Final Chapter

30 years had passed from these stories. Helena had lost Sam who was once her lover. She had left Farhad suddenly 30 years ago and nobody was informed of her during these years! After the death of her husband, Helena had decided to return to Iran… she was looking for those who were not with her anymore. Helena was alone…

The airport hall was very crowded. From the crow who were waiting for their luggage, a pretty middle-aged woman with a beautiful style appeared. She was waiting for her luggage just like other travelers to take it and go towards the exit door of the airport hall. While waiting for her luggage, she got drowned in the past memories. The images of 30 years ago passed in front of her eyes. She did not know and maybe she did not really understand her fate. Life had passed for her like an unbelievable dream!! She did not know what it was and how life had happened to her. She was thinking about those days and the same reality which had turned into a story which was her secret!! Helena's luggage arrived and she picked it. then, she went to the exit door. The airport taxi arrived to the exit door and Helena gave the driver her address. The driver warned her that: Mam, the names of these streets have changed for many years and many people just know the new names but since I'm an old man... and still remember these names, I will take you to your destination. When she got out of the taxi and stood in front of her house with her luggage, she stared at the door for a second!! Her eyes got red. The house where her childhood memories were hidden, the house where she had once experienced love and adolescence, and was forced to say goodbye! And the house where she had lived for many years and had a glorious appearance was now a rusted and old house. When she was standing in front of it, the neighbors were looking at her in wonder and passed her while saying to each other: what if this woman belongs to this house where only rich people can live in!! Helena was looking at the house in wonder and shock. She asked the men in the neighborhood to help her open the house door, so that she could enter the house. When she walked in the yard, suddenly her tears fell down her cheeks and her luggage fell on the ground. She wiped the tears off her face with her fingers and walked towards the house building. The face and memories of Sam came to her mind.

Helena was counting every seconds of those 30 years to come to this house again…

And now her dream had come true and she was feeling happy. She sat on the steps at the entrance of the house. A sad sunset was being formed. She put her hands on her face and cried, cried, and cried…

As she was pulled to herself, it was night and a biter darkness had hugged her. She asked her neighbor to lend her 2-3 lamps to lighten the house and told them that she was the owner of the house!! Her neighbor who was a respectful man took her words seriously and realized that she was abroad and could not remember the streets well. So, he provided Helena with whatever she wanted. Helena thanked that God-fearing and respectful man a lot while she was feeling shy and said goodbye to him and then returned to the house. She changed the lamps one after another and then turned them on. Now, she had realized that the house was full of dust and nobody except the owner of the house would clean there!! She decided to clean the house, the house of her memories... she thought a bit before cleaning every part of the house. She coughed and then laughed. She had just remembered that she was a 50-year-old woman now!! The clock hands showed midnight. After cleaning the house completely, Helena felt tired but more succulent than before. So, she sat in an old sofa and felt happy because of showing her honesty and loyalty to her old house... she breathed deeply, then stood up and went to the window and looked outside. After thinking a bit, she went to her old bedroom and took some rest. She fell asleep deeply... (8:30 a.m.) Helena was startled up with her cell phone ringing (It was Sami, her son on the other side). Sami: Hi. Helena: Hi my son, how are you? Are you ok? Sami: thanks, I'm fine. After a few minutes of talking and getting informed of each other's state, they said goodbye to each other. Helena got ready for another day. She went to the neighbor who had helped her yesterday. She got familiar with the neighbor's wife and they began talking for one hour.

Neighbor's wife: Helena? Tell me about yourself.

Helena: what should I say?

Neighbor's wife: why did you leave Iran and why did you come back?

Helena: It was not my decision to leave my house, my neighborhood, and my country. I was a young girl who had just fallen in love with someone who had taught me honor. A good-looking guy with a pure heart called Sam!!

Fate separated both my father and Sam from me.

Neighbor's wife: what happened to your father?

Helena: My father?! She was imprisoned for the wealth he had collected illegally and after 2 years, he had a stroke in jail and died. This house is the only thing I have because it was under my father's name.

Sam also passed away so weirdly!!

After 30 years, I still wonder how Sam died!!

After losing everything I had in this world, the only person who was left for me was Farhad, Sam's friend. After Sam, Farhad was the only person aware of my pains... we had decided to marry but his father disagreed and since I was alone, one of my relatives who was living abroad suggested me to leave Iran.

I don't know what happened to Farhad. Two years after leaving Iran, I also called him but I couldn't talk to him and this story continued until today that after 30 years, my husband died in that country and I decide to come back here!! And now I'm here with you.

Neighbor's wife: So, you just took the tip of the compass in this story of fate?!

Helena: yes, unfortunately.

Helena said goodbye to the neighbor's wife to go for lunch. She prepared the lunch and decided to go to Sam's grave at the cemetery to get it off her chest what had happened to her after 30 years!! She had her lunch, left the house, and decided to walk on the sidewalk a bit like when she was young and take a taxi when she got tired. As she was walking, she thought how the city had changed! She had been used to those streets and avenues far from crowd with the same simplicity and innocence when people had not been stressed yet because of modern life!!

Helena got tired and decided to take a taxi. She gave the address to the driver and after 30 minutes, the taxi driver dropped her at her destination.

She paid the fare and thanked the driver. Then, she approached the entrance door and went to the information office of the cemetery.

She told them the first and last names of Sam and they also told her the exact place of Sam's grave. She began walking around Sam's grave. As she approached there, she felt the catch in her throat and eyes getting intertwined. She had a strange feeling.

With her tall height and a look full of sad, she stood by Sam's grave…

Except the first look she took at the picture on the grave, she could not look at the picture again.

A head which moved ten times every second and a heart which was full of words as well as closed lips which were silent!

But this silence was heavier than shout!!...

The clock hands were passing each other and the sunset was approaching. Helena asked Sam for forgiveness and left the cemetery.

She was not feeling well but one part of her heart was feeling calm after 30 years and she was feeling a weird relaxation by going to the cemetery. She went to her house. When she entered the house, she drank some water, prepared some food for herself, but suddenly after eating, she felt acid reflux, so she went to her bedroom and lied on her bed. It was 10:00 p.m.

Helena was taking rest that the phone ring startled her up. It was Sami, her son. They said hello to each other and Sami told her that he could get his master's degree. Helena was very happy although she was already aware of it. she congratulated Sami a lot. Sami liked to travel to Iran as always and live with his mother.

He told his mother about travelling to Iran.

Helena left the choice on Sami, so Sami decided to travel to Iran and live in his homeland after consulting his mother. Life is just like a short trip of few minutes inside the cabin of a cable car where you sit and enjoy because of being higher than Earth. You sit there and enjoy the relaxation, but if suddenly you are thrown out of the cable car, you will lose whatever you have and only your soul will remain which is also wounded because of a short-term joy!!!

And the regret of that inner relaxation and joy will be in your heart forever.

8:00 a.m.

The due day arrived and the airport hall was crowded as always. Helena with a bunch of flowers in her hand was waiting behind the window for her only child, Sami. The plane landed on the runway and then stopped on the corner of the runway. The passengers got off the plane one after another.

Sami entered the airport hall. She saw his mother, Helena who was smiling. They approached each other and after saying hi, Helena kissed her son on his forehead and greeted him. After talking a bit, they took a taxi and went home. When they got out of the taxi and stood in front of the house, Helena looked at Sami and then looked at the house door. Helena: my son, this house is the treasure of my past bitter memories when I was young. After entering the house, I want to tell you all of these memories which are related to me and my past, I know you are a kind of man who respect the rights of others whether in their past or now, let alone me, your mother! And I'm extremely happy because of this! Sami took a look at his mother and after listening to all her words, raised his head and continued. Sami: Mom? Don't you want to open the door to enter the house and then tell me about this treasure of your memories?

Helena smiled, twisted the key in the lock, and opened the door.

They both walked towards the house building.

The mother and the son had dinner and talked and laughed that night. Sami went to his bedroom which was prepared by his mother to take rest. That night ended and another morning arrived with a sunlight shining through the window into the living room. Sami rolled around his bed and woke up. He got up and leaned against the door of his room. He saw his mother who was preparing breakfast in the kitchen. Helena: Hi, Sami! Go wash your face and come, breakfast is ready.

Sami: yes, mom. The breakfast table was set and Sami sat on a chair: so, why don't you sit down?!

Helena: I'm not feeling well, no appetite Sami?? You be comfortable…

Sami: No, come here, sit and have your breakfast!!

Helena: Ok, my son, as Iranians say: Bismillah, here you are…

Sami: You don't consider me as Iranian??I've just decided to get employed in Iran and live here.

Helena: perfect! Where do you want to get employed?!

Sami: it would be great if I could teach at a university and be at the service of the people of my country, I don't know, anywhere I can work for my homeland. Helena: That's great sweetie, it can't be any better. They were talking that suddenly Helena felt unwell and went towards the toilet. She vomited what she had eaten!!

Sami: what's wrong Helena? Why are you sick?!

Helena: Nothing darling, I don't know why I have acid reflux when I eat something, and I feel unwell, I don't know why my stomach is so sick. I'm not fine at all, I told you a few minutes ago that I can't eat anything. Sami: mom, we'll go to a doctor today to see what's the problem. I'm scared if this condition is dangerous! We have to go.

Helena: ok honey, we'll go. It was at the noon before the lunch time that they made an appointment with a doctor upon the insistence of Sami. They saw the doctor and he examined Helena. He asked them to have some tests and then come fort another examination. After four days, Helena and Sami went to the doctor with the papers of test. They sat at the office and waited for the doctor to say his opinion and tell them what the problem was?!

Doctor: don't worry, with the modern science everything can be cured.

Sami: Please doctor, explain what is my mother's disease.

Doctor: since in these few sessions, I've realized that you are rational people, it's better to think about the cure as soon as possible.

Helena: please tell…

Doctor: gastric cancer. I emphasize that you have to start the stages of cure as soon as possible.

Days passed and the stages of chemotherapy arrived.

Helena had lost her hair on head and face and it had completely changed her face! Helena was not feeling well on those days and Sami, her only child, was also worried. After 3 months. The doctor recommended Helena to be hospitalized in a cancer hospital to be under intensive care. She had accepted that it was her fate and was also out of her control. She just trusted in God and asked Him to make the best thing happen for her…

Sami was present next to his mother with all of the tricks he knew to keep Helena happy and make her have a good spirit for fighting the disease, but the ruined face of Helena left a painful heart for Sami!!

Sami's only job was feeling sad.

It was 9:00 p.m. and Sami who had not slept well even for one night for a long time, sat on the chair next to the bed of his mother and put his head on his head which was pressing his mother's hand. He fell asleep because of being so exhausted. Suddenly, Helena woke up and awakened Sami too.

Sami: what? Are you awake lovely?

Helena: yeah honey, just go get a pen and paper for me, I need it…

Sami looked at Helena's face!! Sami: Ok, I'll get it.

Sami brought the pen and paper and put them next to his mother. Helena: Sami??

Sami: yes, mom?!

Helena: You know well that I'm not feeling well after 7 months of struggling with this disease, tonight you can see that it's even difficult for me to talk. So let me at least write my will as I tell you the story of my life!! Sami: mommy! Tell me whatever you want and write whatever you want in your will, but remember that you are my only mom and you are the loveliest person for me in this world…

Helena told all of the stories of her young age to her only child and said the reason for separating from Sam as his death and separating from Farhad, Sam's friend, as her travel to the US. She told that she had married Sami's father in the US and lived there until he died and then she decided to come back to Iran!!

Sami was shocked of all the details in this story.

He nodded and continued. Sami: life plays with us so hard! Sami began writing Helena's words as her will and Helena asked Sami to make her grave next to Sami after she died…

Sami continued to the end of the will and then gave the will to Helena upon her request.

7:00 a.m.… Sami was asleep deeply while being tired and distressed and holding Helena's hand in his hand!

Suddenly, he woke up with an inner inspiration. With his first look at his mother's face, he found that she was dead and her soul had flown. Helena's eyes were half-open, her hands were numb, and her head was left on her one side towards Sami as if she had been looking at Sami at the last minute. Helena had gone forever and had entrusted her child to God…

In this way, the story of Helena had ended just like the stories of Sam and Amir Ali.

In the morning of funeral, Sami who was standing in front of the crowd and watching the end of her mother's story had a feeling of fear as if he was dreaming!! He had a natural sense of a weird shock which was unlimitedly sad just like when the world was ended...

Sami had been caught in this sudden feeling!

After one hour that some of the neighbors and relatives had come to the funeral, Sami asked the others to leave him alone with his mother. He had started at the picture of his mother on the grave for a few minutes and thought about her words at the last minute. When he was feeling bitterly, his tears fell down. He wiped the tears off his cheeks with his fingers. Suddenly, he turned his face towards Sam's grave that was nearby. He went towards his grave slowly, stood at his grave, and stared at the graved image of Sam that realized the sweeper of the cemetery was standing near Helena's grave!! It attracted Sami's attention. He ran towards the sweeper and looked at him!! Sami: can I ask what has attracted your attention?! Sweeper: you were not at Sam's grave?

Sami: Sam?!! How do you know Sam? Sweeper: I'm Farhad! I knew Sam 30 years ago. After the death of Sam and Amir Ali, my only real friends, I decided to come here, work here, to be near my friends!! When I saw that you went towards Sam's grave, my attention was attracted to there!! Where you were standing, anyway! Accept my condolences!! Goodbye my son…

Farhad took his sweep, said goodbye to Sami, and began sweeping up the street. Sami who was confused looked at the graves of his mother and Sam, turned his head away, and saw the same old man who was sweeping up along the street. The days of loneliness were passing so heavily for Sami that as if he was carrying a chest full of sorrow and riddle with himself. He did not know how to think?! His only fear was judgment because he was not there 30 years ago to know how this story began or ended! He saw himself stuck in this story but said nothing, so he decided to keep this story full of secrets in his heart forever. A sacred secret called love which is an earthly love according to this young man of modern era but he was a bit unfamiliar with these kinds of secret and they seemed weird to him…

Sami decided to go back to the US to meet his father at the cemetery and mitigate his sorrow and then return to his homeland and teach at the university in Iran as his mother had suggested. Sami's travel took long for 20 days and he returned to Iran with a milder spirit. The first thing he did after returning to Iran was meeting his mother. He went to the cemetery, sat on his knees next to his mother's grave, and stared at his mother's picture, he did not cry or was not sad!!

But he just stared at the grave and after a few minutes, he stood up, took a sad and new look at his mother's picture, and went to the house. As he arrived at the house, he remembered the day his mother was standing next to him, staring at the house door, and Sami was looking at his mother!! He lowered his head, breathed in deeply, and breathed out sadly. Then, he twisted his key in the lock and entered the house. At the moment of entering the house, his face showed that he had a weird feeling in his heart and such a feeling was originated from his look at the yard and building that his mother had enthusiastically told all of her memories in this house. He raised his head and saw the neighboring man and his wife who were standing in the balcony of their house and looking at Sami with their sad faces. They nodded their heads to sympathize with him. Sami breathed deeply and went towards the entrance door of the building. As he entered the house, he looked at the inner space of the house for a few minutes.

With a half-open mouth, raised eyebrows, and a sad in his eyes, he was walking in the living room and then he went to the bedroom, lied down on the bed in a crumpled way, and fell asleep deeply. Hours passed and he was sleeping with his tired body but comfortable far from any chaos.

It was as if he wanted to sleep forever. After 4 hours, he startled up, looked around, and threw a small frame of the picture of him and his smother to the wall and shouted sadly: Why? After a short pause, he went to the mirror in his room, looked at it, and wrote on it with his finger:

Wind-up humans will also die one day…. Wind-up humans will also!! Die one day….

The End

Title: **Yousef's brothers**

A lonely young man is involved with rebellion
Some rebellious men from his tribe
Have put him on fire
Lonely… lonely… lonely
At the end of a lonely pain
He was waiting for friendship and kindness
But the repetition of fire had made him tired
There was no kindness and affection
All paths were deadlock
He had to go…
He had to go far away
Perhaps there is no rebellion there!
I am sad about disability…
Because I could not… I could not!
Sacrifice myself on this lonely way
What did the rebellious men do?
A lonely young man is involved with this rebellion…

Title: **My only friend, my mother!**

The sky was crying
When you were crying
It was whining, it was raining…
When you were putting up with
The sorrow of your children
The sorrow of my loneliness
The endless pain and sorrow of me
I am full of complaints…

You are innocent, oh you the most heavenly
I am the beginning of a bitter end
Why did you feel bitter with my bitterness?!!
When I do not know, why do I exist?
You remember me
Remember my childhood
Remember that this is the world!...
I break my heart for you
Shame on me and this world
My eternal friend
My mother…
I want to say hello again to you
Hello, hello, hello, to my only friend: my mother…

Title: **Aryan land**
There are Medes and Parthians!
My race is from the Aryan immigrants…
Finally, the name of my land is Iran
Iran, my homeland…
I am a part of you
As you are big and as I am so small…
My homeland, Iran
I wish I was alone
I was I was Aryan!!
I would reach my ancestors
While the time passes to the past
Oh my land of attachment
I love you, I remember you…

The eras always pass

Iran…

My homeland

Oh you the wounded land of history

I love you

I love you

Title: **Do not be afraid, my heart… God is with us**

It's me, my pen, and a white paper

The wall has surrounded me from the four sides

This room is very paled without any color

That does not even shout my voice

Murmurs are heard from inside a chest

That nobody is aware of it outside there

How lonely and quiet you are! When you are alone

There is still a relaxation at the end of this loneliness

Chaos, conflict, and game are enough

Hey lonely heart! Put up with me…

I am also like the same broken window

I will not deceive you anymore

It is not the time of rebellion anymore

If it is? The world makes me relentless

Well done to you, my white paper

That bought the ink of my pen as it was

Hello to you the companion of my loneliness

My lonely heart…

Do not be afraid, God is with us

Do not be afraid

God is with us…

Title: **In memorial of the dreams which come and die…**

In memorial of the dreams which come and die

I remain silent, heavier than shout

Where are you Farhad, the mountain carver? My yokefellow

I have learned from you, my lonely friend

To keep my wishes in my chest

There is no muddy wall, silence of the alley of memories

There is no shame and modesty of enjoying life

And there is no arriving simply, or hearing simply

No voice is even heard from the true beloved

Everything is just a lie!!

I will go away, I cannot tolerate

What if my heart, you will be lonely and be cracked?

Do not take my collar… I am lonely too

A broken heart does not need a filled heart

How beautiful the beach is at the time of loneliness!

My friend, I will leave my pains alone with the beach too

Title: **Conversation**

I am sitting and revealing the secrets to myself

I am searching in my loneliness

No way of leaving is a medicine for treatment…

I cannot be left on my own

It is not in my control

I was born from human!

The round earth is spinning weirdly!!

Stones hit our earth inch by inch

What is doing this world?!

Nobody hears the whistle of hearts

When the windows are all closed

What is new from the wandering passer-by who is singing?!

This snow of December does not save us

Conversation was nice in December

Title: **Panacea after Farhad's death**

You are quiet, my friend

As always, but alone…

And how sad I am thinking about you here…

My fall tears had no cure

No! this destiny of not being is not yours

Such a leaving suddenly

The angel of death does not fool anyone

Perhaps, he kills himself not to be alive again

I wish this angel of death gave you a chance

Not to feel ashamed in front of me…

I do not want this destiny

My heart is whining of leaving!

Of my empty luggage

My friend, my cold hands are empty

Another feeling has come to my mind

I am struggling with my situation

And an endless path, my destination...

I do not complain these people

Their emotions belong to themselves

My pain belongs to me

If there is no panacea

There is not even a doctor

I do not complain

This is life, that is is….

Title: **Your presence**

Hey you singing bird

Sing for me a little

Do not avoid, I have lots of complaints in my chest…

I can soar with courage

I have barely wings to fly

When there is a fellow traveler in the sky far from me

In this narrow and chaos world

I got captured when I was looking for peace

If you soar too, I will be lonely…

Hey you singing bird, sing for me a little

My life is colored with your presence

It becomes beautiful with your modesty

I do not understand how I feel

When you whisper to me

In this cage

That we are a companion of each other

One day I am dumb and one day you are silent!

My old heart falls in love easily

It hears easily, understands easily

I wish this simplicity was flowing
I wish this simplicity was running…

Title: **Swan song**
I look at you
And you visualize me simply
I miss you
But you take me to the mirage…
Oh you, beautiful swan!
I'm shouting in a sky
In front of where you are quiet
Your song has made me humble
I am scared of the minutes of leaving!
Your unkindness is like a nightmare
When I know that my mate is the loneliest in the world…
I wish I was not and did not see
I am involved with your peace
You are also a part of it…
One day, you will die too, beautiful swan
Like me, that will leave one day, like you…
Your song is pleasant
Because I hear it well
I am adapted to your song and am tuned to heat it, it !!
The sorrow of the sky is feeling lonely in your heart
Because you are not adapted to it
I understand it, hey you, beautiful swan
I have cried with it, I have laughed with it

I consider you simply

And maybe you visualize me simply

Title: **Thinking of you**

Thinking of you starts an uprising in my heart

The sweetness of those days puts me on fire

My life is bored of impatience

Save me, you the eternal one…

My itinerary is a premature aging

Which has a deep gap between being or not being!

Every minute of it was boring to me

I wish you sat by me at that moment…

Look, there… did you see?!

What children did with their mothers

What oppression they did?

Look there…

What a beautiful flower the orphan kid had in his hand!

I wish our world was white like snow

Like a jungle when it was raining

It had the thirst of being pure again…

You the most eternal one

Be with me…

Stay with me…

Title: **The tradition of our time**

I do not know where I will travel?!

I hope wherever I go is lonely, since I am lonely too

A lover imprisoned in himself dies

If he does not see a lonely night!

Our out of tune instrument plays with the time

Its sound is hot

Hey you the Tombak of happiness, do not come because my heart is wounded

My sighs and whining belong to me!

The bridge of happiness belongs to you have put my head next to my out of tune instrument

So, I am still alive…

Wow… what a tradition is

The tradition of our time…

Title: Hush…. Do you hear it?!

This sound is a familiar sound

That says I am like you and know you

This sound cannot be heard

It must be believed

It is so restless for me

That I do not know why I have neglected it

Perhaps, its house is in the sky

It is the song of freeing from emotions

Which have settled in my heart like a calling

Freeing from body and flying the feelings

When I am with you, I do not see any repetition

Inside me goes around every moment

I fall in love... my eyes get teary

Sometimes, I look at the sky

Do not pay attention to my tired look

Just listen…

The eternity of me and my dearest ones
Is being with you
You the lonely one forever…

Title: **Turn off the lights…**
I am in love with the sky at night
I am the guard of this sky
My attitude to life changes at your presence
My loneliness is gone if someone like you is with me
The pain of the world, like an attractive song
Has made me busy with itself…
The stars in the sky full of affectation are charming
What should I do? I am a high-flying stranger
I wish there was no this ceiling
I wish I was not captive in this body
I wish the answer to twinkling stars was
Empathy! But no hatred or jealousy
Hey you my heart
This is not the tradition of stars
It was you
It was you, my heart
We can think, we can look
Just at the lonely beloved
No! the sky is my friend
It cries with me, it is proud of me
I also cry with it, I am proud of it
Turn off the lights
But the sky is with me!

Title: **Fall leaves**

When I remember you, I will always do that
I walk in the alleys in fall
These passengers who walk on the yellow leaves
Do not know what days you and I had
What memories we made
Now, you and I are far
I remember you and my heart is distressed
And my unconscious grabs me
In my consuming lonely heart
I die and get alive in your memorial
At these gray moments
Your memorial puts me on fire
How soon the moments die and leave me alone
Forgetting you is not my job
No! It's not…
My heart still gets distressed in your memorial in fall

Title: **A closed window**

A closed window is captive in the middle of desert
Waiting and regretting for a beautiful bird
Regret of heart, regret of heart!
Sometimes, when it opens, it's because of the crowd around it
But they know that they are not anything more than a mirage
They have just made everywhere crowded…
I wish the difference between humans
Was not the distance between the window and the mirage
Or the desert to the window

Hearts require more humanity

The lonely window, desert, and mirage

Are enough!

Title: **Far beach**

I do not know what this lonely beach

Knows about me that is so familiar with me

Those small islands, far away

Are sitting lonely like Leili and Majnoon

But the beach, those islands, and I have the same pain…

We know it well

We do not doubt about the relaxation of each other

We touch and caress each other

How beautiful this relaxation is…

How unjust it is…

This remedy which contains loneliness..

This panacea has affected the beach, surrounding islands, and I

What good friends accompany me

And feel me…

I wish I was a drop of water in this sea

I wish I was an island

I wish.. I wish…!

What a nice and beautiful feeling is

Seeing these friends

They were and are my companions…

Title: **Night of life**

How lonely the words pass my mind

We must build our minds again

And see again

And hear again

A new conversation is needed

How cruel the life got un-refreshing

I want a new beginning

A road full of beauty

The past is a piece of crumpled paper in my hands

I am the traveler of the beautiful days of being with you

I wish the past was like this

And I saw you

Hello to you my new life

The one who will celebrate the Christmas

And me, spending Yalda

Are both happy… are both free…

I buy this happiness

I will spend Yalda night with you until the morning

Yeah, we must see again… and hear again…

A new conversation is needed…

Title: **Beloved…**

Do not remain silent, do not stare at my eyes

My sin was falling in love

I speak simply with innocent

Pay attention a bit

I am this and nothing more

I do not want to be something except this
Quiet and singing
I am looking for my lost beloved in alleys
Pay attention a bit
What do you see in me that surprised you
Why are you scared? It is me
Alone, tired, and restless
Do not remain silent, do not stare at my eyes
I am the traveler of night
I am looking for a bite of relaxation
I get tired, I get alone
I feel calm when I see you
You are silent, proud, and smart
But you understand me!
Be kind with me who am lonely
And talk to me
My beautiful mind
What have you made of yourself?
What a pure image you have made of your beloved
How beautiful this feeling is
I love it
I love it

Title: **Let's talk**

I am standing in front of the sea
I have words
With you the unlimited sea
You are cam a bit like calm humans
No! you will be never like them
I wash my eyes with the water of the sea
Maybe, these drops of water
Are the heavenly tears…
I know that the sky is bigger than you a thousand times
How big are your body and heart and how small I am in front of you…
I see myself next to you one day!
When I am very lonely like you, today
When I know that you take a storm of pain
With you everywhere like me
Inside of me whines about his congener
I will come to you
Sea… sea
I see a sea of loneliness around me
I ran away from tricks deceptions
Which broke the waits of wisdom and honesty
These tricks and those deceptions…
Watching your waves has created an indescribable relaxation in body
But there is no place for trust anymore
This trust may cause an early death
In my mind!

Title: **Father, hello…**

A beautiful hello to the beauty of your face and your tired hands

Which taught me the lesson of life…

Hello to your sea-like heart!!

Hello to your sad eyes

Which taught me humanity and confidentiality

Father…

I am a small river

That reach you one day

Be my sea

What if the world turns me into a lonely swamp

I wish I was a sea

What a thing it is

The day I learned: my heart must be like a sea!

My tears fell down my cheeks

Oh you the only friend of me and my mother

A beautiful hello to the beauty of your tired hands

I love you so much

The End

Summer 2020

Table of Contents

MIX
Papier aus verantwortungsvollen Quellen
Paper from responsible sources
FSC® C105338

Printed by Books on Demand GmbH, Norderstedt / Germany